MAKING
CITIES
WORK

MAKING
CITIES
WORK

HOW TWO PEOPLE MOBILIZED
A COMMUNITY TO MEET ITS NEEDS

BASIL ENTWISTLE

Illustrated by Patric Dawe

HOPE
Publishing House
Pasadena, California

Making Cities Work © 1990 Basil Entwistle

Excerpt from "Upon this age, that never speaks its mind" by Edna St. Vincent Millay. From *Collected Sonnets*, Revised and Expanded Edition, Harper & Row, 1988. Copyright © 1939, 1967 by Edna St. Vincent Millay and Norma Millay Ellis. Reprinted with permission.

For information address: Hope Publishing House, P.O. Box 60008, Pasadena, CA 91116

Printed in the United States of America

First edition

Illustrator: Patric Dawe

Cover Design: Michael McClary/The Workshop

Library of Congress Cataloging-in-Publication Data

Entwistle, Basil, 1911-
   Making cities work : how two people mobilized a community to meet its needs / by Basil Entwistle ; with an introduction by Donald E. Miller.
      p.   cm.
   ISBN 0-932727-37-9 : $15.95 — ISBN 0-932727-36-0 (pbk.) : $9.95
      1. Wood, John, 1917-   . 2. Wood, Denise. 1917-   . 3. Volunteer workers in community development—California—Pasadena—Biography. 4. Community development, Urban—California—Pasadena—Case studies. I. Title.
HN80.P33E58 1990
307.1'4'0979493—dc20   89-38023
                                                                      CIP

Table of Contents

v

Upon this gifted age, in its dark hour,
Falls from the sky a meteoric shower
Of facts . . . they lie unquestioned, uncombined.
Wisdom enough to leech us of our ill
Is daily spun; but there exists no loom
To weave it into fabric; . . .
—Edna St. Vincent Millay

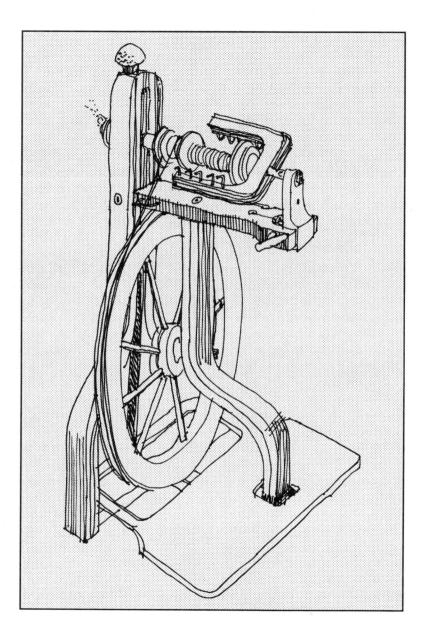

Foreword

This book tells the story of the attempt by two morally sensitive individuals to contribute to their city. Pasadena, the setting for this story, may be the City of Roses, but it still has many of the problems which John and Denise Wood saw when they moved there in 1972.

Yet 17 years later, it also reflects some very concrete manifestations of their service to Pasadena: the Community Skills Center which trains 4,000 people a year, the Commission on Children and Youth which has become a major advocate for the welfare of children in Pasadena and DAY ONE which is addressing in important ways the problem of substance abuse.

Denise's Office for Creative Connections, as well, has been the moving force behind projects ranging from a summer youth employment program to a major initiative regarding health care for low income children. A magnificent celebration of the city of Pasadena's centennial, which John architected, is still talked about. And the list continues.

None of these projects is the sole result of two people's efforts. All involved collaboration and partnerships with many other people. But the leadership, the inspiration, the attention to detail that is essential to any major undertaking came from two individuals who begin each day in quiet reflection, talking with each other and waiting for direction from that power which humbles all who might be in pursuit of personal gain or power.

Although the names "John and Denise" appear often in this book, this is not a biography. Nor is the intention to eulogize the living. Indeed, the modern cult of personality and self-aggrandizement are precisely what the Woods have sought to counter. Their vision has been to think for the *whole* city, to move beyond issues of turf, economic or agency self-interest and protectionism. In the words of social commentators such as Robert Bellah, their interest has been to seek "the common good" as opposed to accepting the ethic of utilitarian individualism which characterizes much of modern life.

In my personal association with John and Denise during the past decade, and now in reading this book, I see a consistent approach to addressing people and problems which is replicable in many other cities, and it is to these principles and methodology of seeking the common good that I now turn. Latent within these pages I find a moral vision that crosses the political spectrum.

It is a conviction that the founders of our nation had, and it is one that runs deeply in our Judeo-Christian heritage. It is a vision that rejects personal self-interest as the ultimate end of life and instead invites citizens to understand that their health, personal and moral, is tied to the welfare of all persons within their community, not least of whom are children and those without hope, skills and dignity.

Nowhere in this book will one find a cookbook formulation of a methodology. Rather, the particular stories, the small and seemingly insignificant events of committee meetings, personal conversations and confrontations between people and interest groups reveal a consistent approach. This vision has been contextualized—validated in action—which is what separates it from being mere superficial moralism. Latent within these pages I see the following principles being enacted.

First, John and Denise are *wonderful listeners*. This is true at two levels. Before embarking on a project they do their research, which is a form of listening by attending to the voices of all parties who are touched by a particular issue. For example, Denise's first significant involvement in the community began by doing a hundred interviews with people at all levels and from all communities within the city.

But there is a second level to their listening, which is what has enabled them to return again and again to people from whom they need assistance. A conversation with the two of them inevitably allows room for your personal hurts, concerns and visions. There is something very pastoral about their interest in people, or might one say very human?

Second, they *refuse to be confrontational*, even though the very nature of the political realm in which they are involved is, by definition, a struggle over power and personal advantage. Part of being good listeners is that they attempt to hear the concerns of persons and groups on opposing sides of an issue and then appeal to "the common good" in seeking a creative solution to an issue or problem.

Political realists will find their approach naïve. And where Saul Alinsky, for example, would organize a march or demonstration, the Woods would invite the opposition over to dinner. It seems like a strange way to do business unless one's vision of human nature allows for the possibility that deep in every human being is a desire to throw off the character armor that falsely protects us from fears about our own finitude.

Third, the Woods have a *bountiful expectancy* that refuses to accept despair or hopelessness. The net effect is that people around them seem to dig a little deeper and find the internal resources to work for common solutions. Cynicism is a word whose meaning they have never learned. They seem to hold a certain anticipation that people would rather do good than evil, if they can only be supported and nurtured in their struggle with the demons of compromise.

Fourth, John and Denise are *honest in their assessment* of people and issues, but they avoid name-calling and blaming. Most of us criticize others because of the feelings of importance and power that it gives to us. The Woods seem to derive their power from another source. Their conviction and analysis of issues consequently have a ring of objectivity and authority to them that provokes others to examine their motives before propounding personal philosophies and programs.

While not exhaustive, these four qualities of character and conviction are, I believe, the foundation on which the various projects described in this book are built. The actual method of their work has focused on creating coalitions and partnerships in which people can seek the common good in their city. In many ways, their contribution to Pasadena has been to serve as the catalyst for bringing people together who share common concerns. What they discovered repeatedly in Pasadena was that there is no absence of agencies or goodwill, but people from parallel agencies or groups often do not know each other, or else never get together to think more broadly about how their individual efforts might be combined to have a more strategic impact on the city.

The Woods' unique role was that they represented no agency or interest group. They could think for the whole city. Their friendships with hundreds of people throughout the city, many of these friendships having been nurtured over leisurely dinners in their comfortable Pasadena home, enabled them to connect and introduce to each other people with common goals and moral commitments.

In addition, they were the moving force behind the formation of coalitions and partnerships which empowered these individuals to seek higher aims than would have been possible had they pursued their own particular goals and ambitions. They did not seek to engineer competitive agencies; instead they sought ways to bring agencies and institutions and individuals into complementary relationships, which on many occasions involved interest groups joining together in common projects.

The social location for a good part of their service to the community was All Saints Church, a large and well-established Episcopal church noted for its integrity and prophetic vision, and symbolically located across the street from the city hall of Pasadena. This was the institution which paid Denise a modest salary for being the director of the Office for Creative Connections and it is also the institution in which John served as senior warden of the vestry.

It is an exceptional church that would offer someone a year's salary to interview people in the city. It is also an exceptional church that would produce laity of the caliber of attorney Bob Denham, journalist Lou Fleming and many others who volunteered their time and professional skills on many projects in which the Woods were involved. The credibility of the church within the community served as the point of reference for much of their work.

John and Denise's vision is a deeply rooted one, anchored in a conviction that moral values are not human inventions, matters of personal preference or personal taste and inclination. It is this spiritual conviction that is the source of power and authority which underlies their activity in the city of Pasadena. Importantly, however, their conviction is seldom expressed in sectarian terms which would only divide rather than unite the diverse constituencies that they seek to mediate and inspire.

Throughout the cities of America, I am confident that there are many John and Denise Woods, people perhaps without formal credentials to renew their community, yet people with deeply rooted moral concerns and a breadth of insight for where they live. Furthermore, there are many churches and synagogues in the city squares of our land with an important enabling role. The stories in this book will inspire and support all those who are potential catalysts for the transforming of America's cities.

—*Donald E. Miller*
Associate Professor of Social Ethics
University of Southern California

Author's Preface

Anyone who reads the morning newspaper or watches evening television news is burdened by the weight of bad tidings. Beyond the daily ration of disasters and calamities there are the headlines reflecting the mounting problems of our society—drugs, crime, ethnic confrontation, child abuse, poverty, unemployment, homelessness. Those of us who are parents and grandparents fear for the future of our young as they grow up in this climate of violence and despair. Many of us have tried to do something to help; we have given money to worthy causes, given time to volunteer organizations, joined protests, written letters, petitioned law makers. Yet we see most problems grow rather than diminish. They seem so pervasive and deep-rooted, even in our own community, that we ask ourselves whether there is anything effective that can be done and what part an individual can play.

So, what is needed? Could it be a different kind of leadership, one that involves more of us who never saw ourselves as leaders; one that inspires, unites and mobilizes a community into action?

The purpose of this book is to describe just such a mobilization in a typical, medium-sized American city. At first sight the two people, husband and wife, who undertook this initiative do not seem especially well equipped to deal with urban problems. John and Denise Wood were certainly not wealthy, not prominent in their community, not trained in social work, not even long-time residents in their city and state. Yet, in the course of the last twelve years, between them they somehow initiated enterprises to which others gave their allegiance and together created structures of lasting value in Pasadena's life, structures affecting job training, children, health and the countering of a rampant drug menace.

The city in which all of this took place is Pasadena, California. Millions of Americans are aware of Pasadena on New Year's Day, when they watch the Rose Parade or Rose Bowl game on TV. It is well known, too, for Caltech, the center for advanced scientific studies, the Norton Simon Museum of fine arts, the Jet Propulsion Lab and the headquarters of the Parsons global engineering firm. But alongside these prestigious institutions and next to its Orange Grove Boulevard and avenues of fine homes stand poor Black and Hispanic areas; old established merchant districts border the new high tech corporations—a mix with which many American cities can identify. Pasadena is also an average sized city and combines a proud independent century-long heritage with its fast growing dormitory-commuting relationship with sprawling Los Angeles.

It seemed reasonable to believe that the Woods' initiative in Pasadena might apply to many cities in the country and I decided to explore what they had done and, perhaps more significantly, how they had done it. After learning from John and Denise all I could about their achievements, I set out to interview some forty of the men and women with whom they had worked—city officials, social workers, educators, clergy, police, heads of community organizations, minority leaders, businessmen and merchants.

My research was enlivened by interviews with colorful characters with whom the Woods were working—a black minister whose house was fire-bombed by a drug dealing neighbor who later asked him and his wife to take care of his children when he went to prison; a psychologist in the police force whose office was stacked with dolls, teddy bears and games for the children he had to remove from violent parents; an able young Hispanic lawyer who found himself, together with Wood, negotiating with city officials against whom he had brought lawsuits on behalf of fellow Hispanics.

What the men and women I interviewed told me pieced together a fascinating picture of a patient human endeavor that had created an effective team. It highlighted certain techniques, strategies and programs. But more important were human qualities that provided the dynamic and cohesiveness needed to mobilize a city to meet its needs. These are the essentials, it seems to me, required by anyone who sets out to improve the quality of life in his or her community.

The problems of Pasadena and the cities of America remain urgent and complex. This book is a blueprint for initiative and action dedicated to those who, like the Woods and their friends, long to play a part in making their community a safer, healthier and better place for all.

*   *   *

I would like to thank those officials and citizens of Pasadena who helped me reconstruct the story of this book. I made many friends in the process. Don Miller as a sociologist has brought his thoughtful perspective in the foreword and Patric Dawe as an architect and artist his finely crafted line drawings to each chapter. I am grateful to Adelaide and Alexander Hixon for their generous contribution toward this undertaking. And finally my warm appreciation to Faith Annette Sand, the editor and publisher who, because of her vision of what the book can mean, added the task of its publication to an already full schedule.

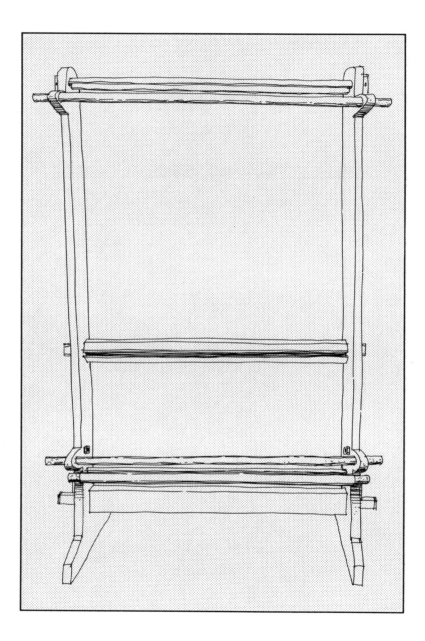

1

Opening the Door to Jobs

Pasadena, California has long been a city with an international reputation. For over a century the New Year's Rose Parade has been a news event that has brought this sun-drenched, palm-lined area of real estate to the attention of millions the world over. It is a city to which the industrialists and bankers who helped boom California's economy go home at night.

And since these power brokers thought of all the details, they joined an east-lying community nestled in the foothills of the Sierra Madre Mountains where the rising sun was at their backs going to work, while the setting sun was behind them as they wended their way back. Thus it is no surprise the Pasadena Freeway, linking it to the heart of Los Angeles eight miles away, was America's first—finished in 1939.

Pasadena is also a cultured city—with the money needed to support art, music and letters and the educational institutions needed to attract world-class scholars and scientists. Here the affluent from the East created their winter estates, building grand mansions with wide, ever-green and manicured lawns. Over the years they established the subtle traditions of a low-profiled elitism that makes popular those places which are little advertised, never-neoned and never pushy. For years one of the nicer public restaurants in town didn't even have a sign outside—its regular customers knew where they were and that was all that was necessary.

But the post-war years brought disruption and the genteel ambience was slowly eroded as Pasadena began to feel the pressures associated with being ten-minutes away from downtown Los Angeles. The exploding immigrant population was spilling into all the empty cracks that appeared, impacting the comfortable life of those who were trying to walk on the other side of the road, eyes averted. Los Angeles began to ooze all around them so that all areas not incorporated into separated towns, like Pasadena, became amalgamated into "The City." Where the refugees from the Dust Bowl years and those demobilized from the Second World War found employment which contributed to the industrial strength, new technology was put in place so that unskilled jobs became scarcer.

The trickle of the poor, near-homeless and hard-to-assimilate-into-society began to grow. Suddenly a stream appeared in the year-round warmth of the San Gabriel Valley. Some settled down and found a corner in the growing job market, contributing hard work and ingenuity to the idyllic valley where it scarcely ever rained. Others never made the right connection and drifted around the edges of society, their anti-establishment stance a worry.

More and more the city's establishment was forced to look into the face of those who were not as fortunate. The social and education systems were obviously not equitable and a growing liberal segment of town began to clamor for "freedom for all." It was therefore not surprising when in the early 1970s Pasadena became one of the first in the nation to implement court-ordered public school busing to make sure the races mixed and equal education was provided to all, causing some more conservative elements in town to flee to neighboring, all-white suburbs.

Soon Pasadena found itself in a predicament no one had anticipated. During the 1970s there was an increasingly serious problem of unemployment, especially among Black and Hispanic young people who, in spite of the reforms, had dropped out of school. Since they lacked the education for the basic skills needed for jobs, some were easy victims for drug dealers and the criminal world, while others were entering a new generation of welfare recipients. Concerned with the inadequacy of available training, educators and city officials on a number of occasions considered the creation of an institution to provide a coordinated job training program for the Pasadena area. A fresh initiative and perseverance were needed.

Then in 1979 a broad-based task force including representatives of three of the city's institutions—the school district, the community college and the city government—began to meet together with a new creative thrust. A year later, to the surprise of many, the Pasadena Community Skills Center opened its doors. Since that day, several thousand previously unskilled whites, Blacks, Hispanics and Asians each year have studied at the center, preparing themselves for a job. How did the "impossible" come to pass?

This was the question Wilson Riles, then California's state superintendent of schools, asked when he was taken on a tour of the center and commented that he could think of a score of cities that would benefit from such an institution. He was told jokingly, but with a kernel of truth, "All it takes is a John Wood."

History is marked by the right people being in the right spot at the right time. At first glance there is nothing remarkable about John Wood in Pasadena. A tall man with an open and gentle face, he and his wife Denise were just two more of the stream of immigrants who had arrived in Pasadena from New York in 1972 because John had taken a job as fundraiser with the Braille Institute in Los Angeles. Both were familiar with the area—John had spent some years in California as a boy—but they were Bostonians by birth, upbringing and accent. Both were in their 50s, yet had married only five years earlier—both for the first time—and had no children.

"When we bought our house in Pasadena," says John, "it was just at the time when families were moving away from the city in reaction to the recent court-ordered busing in the school system. It was a landmark court case in the Western United States.

4

Denise and I said to each other, 'Maybe one day we can have a part in doing something to help turn the situation around. We can't forever keep running away from one another in this world.' "

Accustomed to being involved in community life, they took an active interest in the Pasadena scene and soon learned about the city's racial mix, its areas of affluence alongside others of persistent poverty. They discovered this was a time of intense redevelopment in which great corporations were bringing their imposing headquarters into what had been a somewhat self-contained community where the descendants of small town Midwesterners had settled and done well. Pasadena was now a city of more than 100,000.

The social and economic problems of Pasadena came into sharper focus for the Woods when they joined All Saints Episcopal, one of the largest and most dynamic Episcopal churches in the country. Its rector George Regas, an active, community-minded cleric, was determined to engage the congregation in the concerns of the city. In due course, John was elected to the church vestry and was appointed to a social concerns committee.

For John, this proved to be a momentous choice. In the autumn of 1978 this committee was focusing its attention on unemployment and the need to create jobs as one of the most urgent issues facing Pasadena. The discussion turned to the question of developing a training center to equip youth and adults with skills to enable them to find jobs. John volunteered to research the possibilities of such a center. Knowing nothing about skills centers and little about the problems of education, John decided to go to various people, one by one, who could educate him.

"The person who first came to mind," he says, "was the gifted and sometimes controversial educator, Ramon Cortines. Denise and I had by chance met him at the Los Angeles airport a year before when he was Pasadena's superintendent of schools. We got to know him a little as we sat together flying to Monterey.

"I phoned Cortines and explained my interest. He said, 'Come see me tomorrow, and why not bring Katie Nack with you.' Katie was financial manager of an engineering firm and was also running for the school board. I got hold of Katie, whom I did not know, and I soon learned this was a brilliant suggestion for she would prove to be a decisive factor in the development of the skills center during the next ten years.

"Together we went to see Cortines in his city hall office where he now held a top position in the city government. When I explained I wanted their input on the possibility of creating a skills center, Ray caught fire and talked for an hour. It seemed that it had been his dream. He spoke movingly of school children already losing all hope by the age of nine or ten because of the joblessness they saw around them."

Cortines envisioned a center to which high school juniors and seniors plus adults of all ages could go to be trained in basic skills for entry-level jobs in the Pasadena area. Ray's enthusiasm was shared by Katie, who was shortly to be elected to the school board.

Ray himself was soon thereafter returned to his earlier role as school superintendent.

John left that meeting encouraged at the enthusiasm found in the town's education sector for this idea, and decided to contact leading representatives of the Black and Hispanic communities who would probably be most directly concerned with a learning center aimed at reaching their people. Here he had the advantage of being linked with a church which had made friends in the community and could put him in touch with a wide variety of persons.

One by one he made his appointments. Michael Houlemard, the young Black executive director of the Pasadena Urban Coalition and a graduate of the University of California at Santa Barbara was one of the first. "I immediately liked him," says John, "for his fresh, going-places style and his non-doctrinaire manner in regard to social and economic matters. He knew the needs and was tackling them, but had an open mind about people and about answers. Mike was to become my teacher during much of the coming year and he, too, was in favor of starting the skills center."

So was Nicholas Rodriguez, the aggressive staff attorney for *El Centro de Accion Social*—a mutual assistance organization for the growing immigrant Hispanic population in the Pasadena area. He had gone east to college at Cornell, but because of his Mexican parentage when he returned to Pasadena he could get work only as a janitor. He went on to study law at Berkeley and, though still young, he had made a name for himself by bringing lawsuits, often successfully, against city hall.

"Nico told me that he was living on a salary of $3,000 and living with his mother," says John, "because of his commitment to help his own people. As we came to know him and Houlemard and their wives, they would come to our home for dinner. One thing I have learned through all this—if you are going to make a real difference in a community, you have to try to make your diverse colleagues into lasting friends."

Each of these contacts suggested other people to John and so he continued the process—visiting some dozen representative community leaders. Many of these, John discovered, had long been hopeful of establishing a community skills center, but none of them had ever found the time or the resources needed to get it started. There was an existing vocational training school run by Pasadena City College, but it was considered limited in scope and poorly located.

Other obstacles at that time, John discovered, made it difficult to establish a skills center. The country was entering a time of recession and the city leaders did not relish the idea of generating funds for such a new enterprise. Leaders of the Black and Hispanic minorities, whose youth would be most helped by the center, tended to be very wary of proposals initiated by anyone other than their own. Often they had been disappointed by measures which had sounded promising. Yet, without their full cooperation a skills center would never get off the ground because their people would not take advantage of its facilities.

John decided the time had come for action and he asked the dozen with whom he had been consulting if it would be helpful were they to come together for a meeting. They all answered yes, and they all came.

John recalls, "My social concerns committee at the church, chaired by a discerning person, George Ferrick, had helped me formulate the strategy and encouraged me when I got cold feet. One of them, Robert Denham, an attorney with a prominent Los Angeles law firm, joined me for the meeting. It was now July 1979, eight months after I had first started sounding people out about the viability of creating a skills center."

John asked banker George Mannschreck, with a long record of giving job training to young people, to chair the meeting which was held in his board room. Ray Cortines, as school superintendent, told of his vision for a skills center. Then Katie Nack, representing the board of education, came forward with a bold proposal.

The Pasadena Unified School District offered its finest unused property—the centrally located site of the former McKinley Junior High School—free of rent for a skills center, if Pasadena City College would provide the administration and the instruction for the center. Dr. Stanley Gunstream, vice president for instruction at the college, responded that the college was ready to negotiate with the school district to establish such an agreement.

It was clear to John that some significant moves of which he had been unaware had been under way since the calling of the meeting. "At this point in the meeting," says John, "I was conscious that Mike Houlemard of the Urban Coalition had not yet turned up. I felt deeply that his voice in the meeting was important if the community was to pull together over this. So I slipped out and phoned his home—it was still early in the morning—and found that his car had broken down. With my encouragement he turned up in a few minutes. Together with others at the table he was given his chance to express his convictions."

The meeting was affirmative from the beginning to end. It was representative of a community starting to move, to make commitments, to take action toward something they wanted—a community skills center. Within a few days both Nico Rodriguez and Mike Houlemard wrote strong letters to the superintendent of schools expressing the support of the people they represented for the project plus offering to give their own time and efforts to the process of designing the center. The next step was for Cortines to use his position of leadership as superintendent of schools to name a task force that would conceptualize how the skills center should be set up, organized, funded and administered, as well as set the scope of its responsibilities.

Even though attempts to accomplish something like this had been made in the past, they had all ended up as pieces of paper with no action and increased skepticism, because no one had taken the time to lay the necessary ground work between the three governing bodies—city, public schools and college—so that they would all regard this project as their own. It was now clear that all of their participation had to be secured if the project was to get under way.

"For several weeks," John remembers, "there was no action from Cortines who was engulfed in other school problems. I was determined to keep the momentum going and to see that Mike's and Nico's offers to help should not go unanswered, so I invited Katie Nack to lunch, together with Bob Denham, where I expressed my concern. During our conversation I was glad to hear that Katie had been struggling to see that Cortines' appointments to the task force would not be routine, but rather that he would assign decision-making people to the task."

Looking back several year later, Katie Nack recalled, "One of the major objections that had to be overcome was the understandable attitude of the college that resisted a cooperative effort—it basically wanted a new house for the program from which it felt it was being displaced. The school district also had doubts. Our only reason for being involved was to have some training for our eleventh and twelfth graders. Proposition 13 had just been passed in California making deep cuts in the school finances. To have another source of training for the eleventh and twelfth graders was the carrot for us. It was not an undertaking to be easily solved."

A few days later Cortines announced the task force and, to John's complete surprise, asked him to chair it. Feeling his lack of experience in such a venture, John said he would undertake the job if Cortines would name Denham, the attorney, as vice chair. Cortines also named Katie Nack to represent the school board, John Crowley, who had long had hopes of a skills center and who was to prove to be a stalwart protagonist for it, to represent the city board of directors (which is Pasadena's equivalent of a city council), Stan Gunstream to represent the college, and Mike Houlemard, Nico Rodriguez and the banker George Mannschreck to represent different communities of Pasadena. Cortines also included five other representative and able people.

Reflecting on the responsibility given this task force, John comments, "Cortines' charge to undertake such a tripartite venture was something that no other city in California had aspired to or succeeded in accomplishing. Here was an assignment that was bigger than me, maybe bigger than any other individual on the task force to handle. I would have to draw forth the wisdom, the know-how and the will of my colleagues to make it happen. I could see that my job would be to listen, to encourage and to help us all to persevere."

John called the first meeting of the task force within a few days of the appointments and from then on they met once or twice a week at 7:30 in the morning for four and a half months in one of the All Saints' rooms just across the street from city hall. John says he turned first to Mike Houlemard and Bob Denham to advise him on how to organize the task force's efforts and delegate responsibilities. Mike he asked to draft the statement of need for their report because he wanted the pain of 30% (or more) unemployment among Black and Hispanic youth to be emphasized.

"Representative and able these task force members were," says John. "Of one mind they were not. We were coming from different places and so our views clashed and at times our patience would run out. A prominent member of our force lost heart halfway through, feeling that we wouldn't succeed, and gave up on the assignment. I had to bring in a replacement quickly to keep his work going."

John paused a moment, "To be quite honest, I myself had qualms. One day lunching with Bob Denham I asked, 'Do you think we're going to make it, Bob?' Fortunately, he remained hopeful. As I look back now, I realize how essential it was to take the time to 'hear' each other during those weeks, and to learn from one another. We never took a vote. There was never a majority decision over a minority. On every issue we were, at the end, of one mind and we came to a full agreement unanimously on everything."

Finally the task force presented a simple but challenging proposal for a tripartite understanding: 1) The Pasadena Unified School District was to turn over free of charge the valuable, but unused site—the former McKinley Junior High School—for the student center. 2) Pasadena City College was to furnish the center's administration and faculty, drawing on the funding provided by the state of California for non-credit students enrolled at a community college. 3) The city of Pasadena was to serve as a channel for federal funding of capital improvements, for job placement and for community support.

This novel cooperation was accomplished, Katie Nack recalls, "largely because of John Wood who was able to bring to these bodies—who didn't always agree with each other—an objectivity that forced us to think of the whole and bring the skills center into being."

Dr. Gunstream of the college agrees: "We each had our independent goals. From the college's point of view, we were already doing, with our adult vocational school, what the others were now attempting. At the start I felt that the college could achieve the aim of the group by ourselves, as far as education was concerned. Then the political reality sank in and I realized the others *were* needed. Our school could not incorporate the large numbers of jobless and drop-out high school students already in the community. I had to back up and become sensitive to the attitudes of the others.

"In this milieu John Wood was a low-key personality, not excitable and able to meld the various groups together and come up with something that would be workable. It was essential that all three parties felt they had done something constructive. Because of his leadership John was able to attain that cooperation. The skills center would not have come into being without the board members of each of those three groups becoming turned on."

Nico Rodriguez, now an attorney in one of Pasadena's largest law firms, reflects on the significance of what was accomplished: "The decision-making in which we were involved is by its nature a very political process, and for the most part it's governed by people who work in their self-interest—for their personal or group's economic advantage. Those of us on the task force were no exception. In recent years in Pasadena there has been a lot of conflict in decision-making areas—administrative complaints, law suits, plans that die in developmental stages because of political opposition. And nothing gets done until you have people like John and Denise, whose motivation, as I perceive it, has been truly directed to transcendent values of the community, even at the expense of their own personal economic benefit.

"I entered the task force as one who was a critic of the city's implementation of what they call manpower programs, with federally funded job and training programs. On behalf of the Hispanic population, I had written a number of challenges to the city's program. My analysis was that the city used the manpower programs as political favors. For example, a trade union that was contributing to a number of political campaigns in the city was receiving a rather large grant from these manpower funds. It was my belief that there needed to be a major overhaul of how the programs were run.

"So, on the task force you have me on one side of the table, as a critic, and on the other, people who were responsible for running the programs. It's pretty hard to engage in a dialogue when you have that kind of a forum unless you have somebody who is respected, with command presence, with impeccable integrity who will facilitate somehow your being able to reach some kind of agreement or consensus. The fact that we came out of it with something everybody bought into and approved of—well, the unanimity of the task force was a miracle."

A decade later another member of the task force, Michael Houlemard, described those strenuous meetings. "I was at the time with the Urban Coalition and met John Wood at what was the start, I suppose, of his community involvement in the city of Pasadena. This is a mini-metropolis with a little bit of everything—a growing Salvadoran community, a strong Hispanic community larger than the Black population, and a growing Asian community. Along with this multi-cultural mix, there are all the problems of a metropolis. John, a thought-provoking person, was already looking at these things at the end of the 70s. Instead of just expressing his own convictions on that task force or taking a position, John asked questions that made us all think.

"The main confrontations on the task force," Houlemard recalls, "came from the questions of how to get people to participate in the skills center, then deciding where it was to be located and also where the funding was to be found. Nico Rodriguez and I shared a lot of convictions. Both of us were in our mid-20s and many of the people we'd grown up with had skills and talents like ourselves but didn't have the opportunities to get a job or a position. They weren't as fortunate as Nico and I were to get employment. So there was a lot of fighting on our part during those sessions to make sure the young Hispanics and Blacks in the Northwest and North-Central Pasadena could have the break they had been long denied.

"For this reason the location of the building was a very hot issue among us. One question was whether the McKinley School was really a suitable site for young Blacks and Hispanics, since it had been an almost entirely white school. There was a strong opinion among some members of the committee that the center should be in Northwest Pasadena, where so many of the Blacks and Hispanics lived. The way we solved the controversy was to design an outreach program to go out and seek the people for whom the skills center was intended. Everybody wound up in agreement."

Houlemard also mentioned John's continuing influence on the development of the community, noting his skill over the years in asking questions from the various people he meets which has made Pasadena think about itself. John had influenced the community's self-perception and its subsequent actions, stimulating an active involvement in the governing process.

"There is both good and bad in participatory government," says Houlemard, with a grin. "It slows the process and makes it difficult to do things in the most economical way—it costs the city and developers more money. But in the end you come up with a higher quality product, something you can be proud of and live with and support. That's how it was with the skills center."

A much respected trustee of Pasadena City College, attorney Walter Shatford, sums up the accomplishments of the committee. "The three governing units," he says, "each had their turf to protect. There had long been tensions between the groups. To bring such competing factions together and get them to cooperate was no small enterprise."

But it is fair to say something was at work to enlist these diverse and energetic individuals to trust themselves to a process rather different from usual committee work and not to rely on a motion carried/ motion defeated process, but rather to search out the wisdom and the realities in differing points of view, while holding central the essential task needing to be done.

As for his part, John said to Denise one morning at breakfast, "I didn't know I had it in me to bring it together." She looked at him thoughtfully, for by now they had begun to realize that most people are capable of doing a lot more good for their communities and making a difference to all those around them than is imaginable. A vital ingredient is a willingness to try and become involved in being a problem solver. Certainly Denise and John have observed this factor in their own lives.

2

Four Thousand Trainees a Year

At 72 years of age John's Old School training shows in his erect bearing, his modulated Bostonian accent and his gracious demeanor. Denise appears his perfect companion, tall, dignified and someone you immediately feel is trustworthy. She is also a wonderful storyteller with an accent honed from having a French mother and a Bostonian father. The two met when John was at Harvard and Denise at Vassar, but instead of marrying then and settling down to a comfortable and professional life-style, they both were caught up in trying to make a difference in their worlds.

While undergraduates they had both encountered an international enterprise whose goal was to work for peace and justice around the world, especially with government and industrial leaders. When they graduated from college both John and Denise became involved in this world-wide program.

Denise went to France which was recoiling from the effects of the Second World War and there she devoted her energies with others to help bring about reconciliations between those who had long lived with enmity. John, after being demobilized from the army, rejoined the program and worked in Europe and later in North Africa, Asia and South America. One year led to another, one project to another, and even though their paths occasionally crossed, it wasn't until they both were over 50 and traveling as educators with the enthusiastic young singers in the "Up With the People" project, that they decided to marry and at long last settle down and find roots.

John and Denise would never have thought of Pasadena as a place to start, but a job offer and a variety of circumstances brought them to this community—which had many of the same needs for reconciliation as had war-torn Europe or the deprived Third World countries where they had worked. Still, as most people, they never expected to make that much difference in their new community.

But old habits sprang up, and not too surprisingly they soon found themselves enmeshed in projects trying to make Pasadena "work." This history also explains why John was soon regarded as a catalyst by the small group of Pasadenans who found themselves trying to establish a skills center. John was surprised that he "had it" in him to bring off such a project, but his whole life had been based on a profound secret: When a group of not-too-confident people see a job that needs to be done or a civic problem that should be addressed, by dedicating themselves to finding a solution and working together, they often surprise even themselves.

This was certainly true of the skills center project. And since success breeds success, as these concerned citizens on the task force watched the results grow of their cooperation and dedication, they were not only invigorated, but they were also spurred on to try newer and grander projects.

So when the preliminary commitments to establish a skills center were over, the task force had reached agreement on what the mission of each of the three groups should be. Now came the crucial work of seeking the agreement of the city, school district and city college to their recommendations.

On March 11, 1980 John Wood and Bob Denham formally submitted their report to the superintendent of schools. It made a specific proposal for joint action by the three bodies in the form of an identically worded resolution by each. Ray Cortines was delighted with the document which empowered him to approach the three governing bodies with a far-reaching proposal. Since individual members from each board had participated in the task force and had kept their colleagues aware of the progress, these bodies were alerted and prepared for action. Within four weeks three identical resolutions had been officially adopted and a partnership established—the first such in California.

Amazingly, in five short months—by September 1980—the skills center opened at the McKinley site with 1,200 students enrolled, soon to become 3,500 a year. On November 10 Jack Birkenshaw, staff writer for the *Los Angeles Times*, reported on an interview with the center's director, Dr. James Crayton, under the headline, "Job Hungry Flock to Skills Center":

> Pasadena—The Community Skills Center, which opened this fall, soon may be the most popular school in town. The center, which occupies the former McKinley Junior High School site on South Oak Knoll Avenue, provides job training for 1,200 students.
>
> A number of classes have waiting lists and demand for new classes would exhaust available space. "We didn't anticipate the demand would be so great," said James Crayton, center supervisor.
>
> He credits the center's popularity to its central location and classes that offer the promise of prompt employment. Minorities make up most of the enrollment, although Crayton said there is "a good ethnic mix." The mix is evident in the serious faces of the students—Latinos, Asians, Black and whites—as they work at keyboards, sewing machines, engines and electronic components. Where needed, students are required to take basic reading and writing and English-as-a-second-language.
>
> "We offered 20 such English classes at the start of the semester and it has now increased to 40," Crayton said. The classes are offered at the center and at other locations around the district.
>
> Among the classes being requested are bank teller training, masonry, small appliance repair, printing and telecommunications. Space is the urgent problem facing the center, Crayton said. Classes such as

drafting and electronic assembly require considerably more space than just students' chairs.

Most students are in their 20s and 30s, although ages range from 18, the minimum without special permission, to the 60s. There are no entry requirements.

Superintendent Cortines said he sees the center as a hub in the community, a place for basic education (reading and writing) and job counseling and training, involving the Pasadena Chamber of Commerce, industry and business. . . . Joseph Zeronian, district business manager, said, "None of us have been in this kind of program before and there are few models. It's being developed as we go along."

Joyce Ball teaches key data entry, "where the computer starts," she said. She has 52 students and a waiting list of 20. "We can't fill all the jobs available," she said.

A popular course, and one that leads to immediate employment, is power sewing, making clothes and draperies, said instructor Marina Hinds. "We have more job offers than we can fill." Employers are mainly clothing manufacturers in the San Gabriel Valley and Los Angeles.

In a classroom that looks like a small supermarket, Glen Wilkerson teaches merchandise and checker training. "The left hand is on the keyboard of the cash register and the right hand moves the merchandise," explains Wilkerson to student checkers waiting on other students playing the role of customers. Twenty 'ring-ups' a minutes is the goal. Job opportunities are good for grocery checkers, Wilkerson said, and pay starts at $5.21 an hour.

Earl McClanahan, 75, is a substitute art teacher at the center. His popular class can lead to a commercial art career. The motorcycle repair class begun at an earlier site has placed 70 students in jobs and "I could place another 50 if I had them ready," said instructor Mel Mayfield. Sisters Maria and Gloria Rodriguez of El Monte plan to open their own repair shop when they complete the two-year motorcycle repair course. "It's not difficult to learn; it's interesting, and you can always wash the grease off," Maria said.

In December, 1982, a little more than two years after the center opened, an educator evaluated its work in a letter published in the *Star-News*:

As a resident of Pasadena I wish to express gratitude for and pride in a recent and quite remarkable factor in the life of the city. I teach a graduate course in International Education at the University of Southern California. Of the 20 students in the class, 14 are from the Middle East, Latin America and Africa. In order to demonstrate an innovative approach to education I arranged for them to visit Pasadena's Community Skills Center.

It was an intriguing evening. We found a beehive of activity. People of all ages were intensely preoccupied with learning because it was directly related to their survival and advancement. Studies ranged from English-as-a-second-language to completion of high school to practical up-to-date vocational skills. Even more important was an all pervading atmosphere of job expectancy.

This was not only evident in the active job placement office but on the classroom bulletin boards showing where graduates were now employed.

As my students and I listened to Dr. James Crayton explaining the origins and functions of the skills center, I realized that we were hearing something unique. Yes, there are adult schools everywhere. But here was a training ground run by the school district, the community college and the city which had been conceived and planned by a community task force of citizens representing all aspects of the city including minority groups, business, education and private life. When the skills center came to birth it did so because of the persistence, sensitive and unselfish planning process of that task force.

Seven thousand students go through the center in a year. In the present perspective of 12 million Americans unemployed, I believe we have something in Pasadena that can serve as a model for other parts of the country.

Indeed, one of my students from Mali, Africa, who is pursuing his Ph.D. in Education Planning immediately began to think of its application to his own country. I believe this center can serve as a model.

My thanks and congratulations to Pasadena and especially to those who have made the skills center work. It is a center of pride for all of us.

—*W. Tapscott Steven, Jr.*

By the summer of 1988 there had been some changes in the composition of the student body and in the curriculum, but Dr. Crayton as director would still point to the quality and dedication of the teachers as one of the great assets of the center. Working sometimes under difficult circumstances they went the extra mile.

Typical of the best of the faculty is Noemi Garcia, who has been teaching electronic assembly since the skills center was opened. Short in stature, she moves and speaks swiftly and has an enthusiastic, no-nonsense approach to life. Noemi welcomes visitors to her two adjoining classrooms, filled with work desks where she teaches electronic assembly.

"Those first day were hectic," she recalls. "All we had was tables and soldering irons. As more materials came, I set up assembly lines of students re-wiring old equipment and setting up the work boards I had persuaded companies to donate. But that first class was great—90 percent of them were hired and they are all doing well." She walks past rows of photographs of her alumni, and points at one of them. "When that young man first came here the only job he had been able to get was cleaning rest rooms. He had a drug problem. Now he's been five years with an engineering firm and he's doing fine. Learning a skill here changed his life."

Hers is an international class, Mrs. Garcia says, pointing to pictures of young people from Cuba, Colombia, Egypt, Russia, India. "It's a growing family," she says, beaming. "And so many of them are followed by relatives. Nearly 100 percent of them get jobs. Five of them have master's degrees—that man from India and that one from Mexico."

Teaching is only part of her work. She calls on companies such as General Dynamics and McDonnell Douglas and makes friends with hiring personnel. They then phone to tell her of job openings for her students. She also begs for teaching equipment and parts from these companies, and trains her alumni to do the same. The skills center does not have the funds to supply all she needs, but most memorable of her accomplishments is the personal attention she pays to her students—while in her class and after they have graduated.

"Now, here's a fine young man," she says, tapping a photo. "Jose Alonzo is at McDonnell Douglas. They have big plans for him. His supervisor has an eye on him. Like with all my children, the electronics assembly gave them a job. But as with Jose, many of them go on from that to bigger goals. I keep them up-to-date with brochures on technical classes at city college and other schools. Many of them come back here to see me. It's a family and a bond grows between us and especially alumni who now have jobs in the same company."

Jose Alonzo is probably typical of many of Noemi Garcia's students. "If it wasn't for this skills center," Jose says, "I don't know right now what I'd be doing. My sister-in-law told me about it. 'You've got nothing to lose,' she said. 'You don't have to pay anything. Just try it.' I couldn't believe it and said, 'Oh, no, they're just a bunch of rip-offs.' But I went anyway. I'd been going to a state college and I was real discouraged. The instructors just didn't seem to care and I dropped out. I didn't have any skill and I couldn't find a job. So it was at the center that I got all my training. And more than that, I got my self-esteem. I said, 'I can do this. I can do that. I can do anything I want.' "

Alonzo tried various jobs and then landed up at the aircraft company, McDonnell Douglas, as an electronic technician. "I have a good reputation there. People say to me, 'I don't know how you do it.' But I do. I take pride in my work. I like to do a beautiful job. Just today a young woman working on a board near me did it all wrong. The lead person said to me, 'Come here. Do this for her.' I said, 'Yes, ma'am,' and went ahead and did it. Some of the young ladies said to me, 'You shouldn't do other people's jobs.' But I answered, 'No, we're being paid to do the company's work.' I take pride in it. That's something I have learned from Mrs. Garcia. I like to get back and see her and when I visit the center I try to help them with some of the latest techniques we're using at work."

Mrs. Garcia points to the picture of a young Black. "Ron Jones was a school dropout," she says. "He had one of those odd haircuts, wore earrings. He's a big muscular type. When he stared at you he looked fierce. By the time he finished the classes his whole appearance had changed, and his attitude too. I tried to get him a job at McDonnell Douglas. He was turned down there and at several other places. He came in one day and I said to him, 'You look big and fierce. When you go in to apply for a job, you must smile—you have a beautiful smile. Now, go right back to McDonnell and tell them you are really interested in working for them. Keep going back.' Next time he came in he had a grin from ear to ear. I knew what happened. He's doing very well there. There must be at least 30 of my students at McDonnell now. I tell each group that goes there, 'Your behavior and your attitude open the door for the next group.' "

Ron Jones lives in the Northwest area of Pasadena. He was a linebacker on the high school football team, but dropped out of school in the twelfth grade and could not find a job. In 1983 he started at the skills center, also studying electronic assembly and was employed by McDonnell. "Mrs. Garcia's like a mother to me," he says. "She gives me that extra boost. I'm getting ready to go to PCC (Pasadena City College) for a technical degree. The sky's the limit."

Not all students are young. When Julie Bryant entered the skills center in 1982 she had seven children—the two oldest girls in high school. "It was one of them who talked me into going," she says. "She was attending a class in nurse's training at the skills center while still in school. I was really bored, felt empty, wanted to do something for myself besides run the home."

The center runs a child-care center which it uses to train students in child care as well as to take care of the young children of students in classes. So Julie was able to bring her two youngest there while she studied to be a market checker.

"Mr. Wilkerson, my teacher, was in touch with Boys supermarket and they employed me when I completed the course. It has worked fine for me. I work there part-time, and can have time with my family. Also, right now it brings in needed income, because my husband injured his back and can't work."

Among the thousands of youth who have come from Latin America and Asia to settle in the

Pasadena area since the skills center opened is Nancy Aquino, a young woman in her early 20s, who arrived with her family in Pasadena in 1984. "I came straight from school and I found I didn't have enough English language to study in college or to get a job. In 1985 I heard about the skills center and enrolled in an English class. It was a great help to me to practice my English. I was able to do some work in the office at the center and improved enough to be able to study advanced English at PCC. The center helped me too in learning secretarial work. Then the placement counselor told me about this job at Home Savings, where I'm now doing data entry work. Life is very different for me."

The small circle of concerned citizens that began meeting together in 1980 because they were convinced Pasadena needed to help their young people develop employable skills were among the most astonished at how effective their attempt had been. Eight years after the skills center opened the institution was well established and regarded as an important asset of the city. Each year thousands of students were passing through the center and, happily, the great majority who sought jobs after graduating were able to find them.

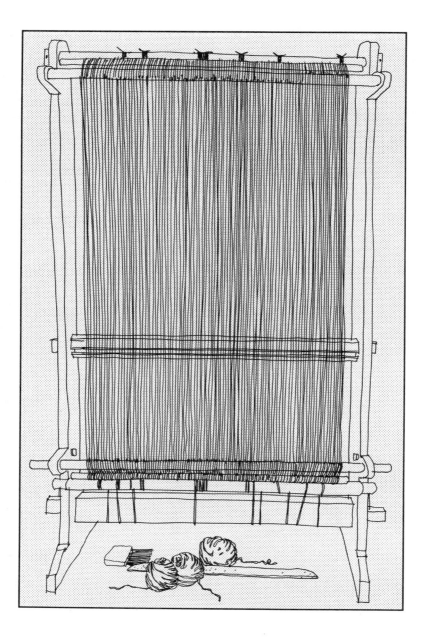

3

An Unprecedented Coalition

This road to success was not without bumps and obstacles that had to be overcome along the way. When organizational weaknesses occurred that began causing a slackening of momentum and a blunting of priorities, it became obvious that something more was needed if the skills center was to keep abreast of the growing needs of the community.

The original task force report had called attention to the need for a mechanism to achieve the necessary coordination at the upper levels of leadership. It recommended that as an initial step John Wood, the task force chair, convene a meeting of the three chief executives (the superintendent of schools, the college president and the city manager), which he did within a few weeks of the opening of the center.

John recalls, "Then I made a mistake. Thinking that the three could carry it on their own, I turned over my leadership of the group to one of them. But these three very busy people simply were not ready for one more commitment and after one or two more meetings, there were no more. I think we all had underestimated the distancing that had grown between the school system and the city government under earlier administrations. So the skills center had to be carried forward by a newly forged cooperation at the working level."

But two years later, the need for top level coordination became acute. The second half of the $400,000 federal grant for the modernization of the center's buildings was being held up because joint decisions as to the long-range plans of the center were not being addressed. Finally John Crowley, then on the city board of directors, phoned John Wood to say that they planned to set up a joint committee made up of two members from each of the three boards provided they could find a disinterested citizen trusted by the three parties to serve as chair. Would John accept the post?

John, feeling a responsibility to make the center work in the most productive way possible, at once agreed and again was thrust back into the middle of the decision-making process.

Shortly after this the tripartite governing bodies created a joint policy review committee. Each of the three boards passed identical resolutions for this purpose in which they stated that "it now appears desirable and appropriate to establish a joint body of representatives of each of the three public juris-dictions, augmented by a well-known citizen as a seventh member who would serve as chair to review accomplishments over the initial two-year period of operation, to identify needs and opportunities, and to report back to their respective boards." It was resolved that each board appoint two of its members on the committee and that John Wood serve as chair.

This arrangement of a joint committee has worked splendidly for over six years, says John. "Meeting every two months or so, sometimes more frequently, committee members have tackled policy questions and common problems head-on in a frank and friendly manner. They have been able to leave turfdom behind and look at questions from the vantage point of the city as a whole. I have great respect and affection for them all. My role as chair has been to give a minimal but necessary amount of leadership, most of all getting the members talking and listening to each other. The creativity and resourcefulness comes out of them. What took many months to iron out before can often now be settled in thirty minutes of honest talk."

This joint committee has been a valuable asset in the opinion of Warren Weber, who was named one of the two representatives to the committee from the city college, of which he is a trustee. Weber, a business person, says, "The members of the committee communicate with each other across the sometimes conflicting interests of the city, school district and college. We are in a fortunate position to do so because our committee is advisory. We do not decide policy; policies are decided by the bodies which we represent. So our meetings are not conducted in the glare of publicity which sometimes encourages people to posture and take strong political positions. There has been much more cooperation at our level than there sometimes is at the staff level of our three agencies, where they feel they have turf to defend."

Virtually all the substantive recommendations the committee made to the three boards have been carried out. Further, says Warren Weber, the existence of the joint committee has brought together people active in Pasadena and other communities who did not know each other. As a result they have been drawn into a cooperative effort in the different spheres from which they come—business, education, civic affairs—for the mutual benefit of their cities.

"But I must go back," Weber explains, "to the work of a few in the original skills center task force. I credit a great deal of the success of the whole undertaking to their insistence on cooperation. It's not normal for agencies to share, as ours have learned to do!"

In January 1989 the skills center faced a second crisis. Due to a number of circumstances, Pasadena City College over a period of six years had seen three different people occupy the post of president. Despite the policy priorities championed by the policy review committee, the in-house chain of command from the top of PCC to the leadership of the skills center lacked clarity. Momentum was slackening, relatively few new occupational classes were being offered, and the center was in danger of becoming a well-meaning institution, not one sharply focused to meet the city's mounting employment problems. Some of the city directors were questioning the center's effectiveness.

Also a difficult issue was coming to center stage: in two year's time the school district would probably have to ask the center to move to another site. Who would lead the search for a new site? Who would rally the funding needed? Only a very viable institution could hope to weather such a transition.

Realizing that the skills center coalition might fall apart, John Wood assessed the situation. He sensed that the new PCC President, Jack Scott, was a person of strength who could face up to realities. Moreover, he had recently streamlined the chain of command between himself and the skills center, placing one of his most energetic and able deans into the key position. In effect, Scott was bringing the skills center into the heart of the college community.

A variety of new occupational classes were introduced and more were being readied for the fall along with an outreach program to young people on the streets and to others who could benefit from the training at the center. More than 4,000 students were now enrolled, but the effect of these new positive moves was yet to be felt in the community.

John Wood decided that Scott could and would turn the situation around but that he needed to know the extent of the doubts surfacing in the community so he could face these directly. Going to see the city manager, John skipped all small talk and went straight to the point, "Do you believe the skills center is doing its job?"

The city manager shook his head, "No."

Then having heard about a new federally funded job training program designed for welfare recipients which was soon going to be assigned, John asked, "Will the city give the skills center a prime role in operating these programs for this area?"

The city manager gave John a straight look, "Let the skills center show us that they can do the job and we will. If they don't, we won't."

Going back to Scott, John relayed these blunt words. An opportunity to stay on the cutting edge of what the community needed would slip away unless some firm, swift action took place to restore city hall's confidence in what the center could do. "I believe in what you and your staff can do with the skills center," John said, "but I urge you to go and see the city manager personally and tell him what you will do."

Dr. Scott, stating that he preferred having questions and criticism out on the table where he could address them, met with the city manager and the school superintendent. Some weeks later he addressed the city board of directors, the board of education and his own board of trustees. All three boards, acknowledging that circumstances dictated the necessity for enlarged and enhanced skills training programs, reaffirmed their commitment to the community skills center.

A new chapter of effectiveness and outreach was starting. It coincided as well with John Wood stepping down after twelve years as chair of the joint policy review committee. He was succeeded by a new and gifted educator, Dr. Ed Shutman, who recently had chaired the Pasadena Human Relations Commission.

Each board gave John Wood their highest commendation and heartfelt words of thanks, acknowledging that the skills center could not have started without genuine communication between those creating it—the same quality of vigorous give-and-take which was as essential ten years later to meet the changing realities affecting the community.

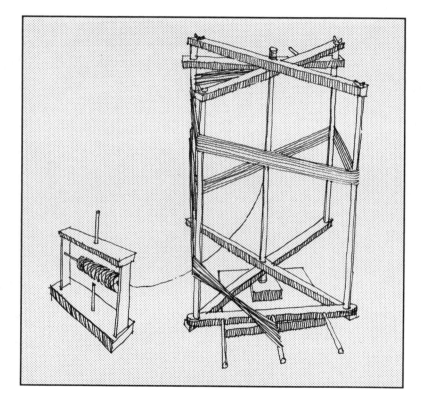

4

From High Rises to Crack Houses

In the early days of the skills center when it was gathering headway, John Wood found himself becoming involved in a leadership role in other areas of the community's life. The skills center had opened in a time of major change in the mood of the city—which was later described by a citizen who played an important role in that reformation, William Bogaard, a banker and attorney who served in the city council and became mayor in the mid-1980s.

"We went through a difficult time in Pasadena," Bogaard says, "in the early 1980s, when there was a substantial reëvaluation of the community's goals. During the preceding decade the primary emphasis of Pasadena, as far as government was concerned, was the revitalization of the downtown area. Now new members had come on to the city council and they reflected a concern in the community that that priority had been sufficiently served. The program of revitalization had, in fact, been extremely successful, but there was a feeling at the time that other community needs were being ignored.

"So, during the first half of the 1980s we saw a multiplicity of goals, which included support for a strong business economy, but which also took into account such concerns as job creation for all Pasadena residents, neighborhood preservation, a commitment to our historic and architectural heritage, and also business development in the neighborhoods of the community. I believe this difficult transition of objectives was accomplished with considerable success."

John Wood was drawn into a growing storm brewing in the community—and which blew up in the autumn of 1980—over the rapid rate of high-rise development in the city's downtown area. The chamber of commerce had promoted an economic development program designed to create industrial sites, attract new industry, business, conventions and tourism, as well as strengthen retail trade. During the 1970s large corporations such as the world-wide Parsons engineering company had located their headquarters in downtown Pasadena.

A powerful organization had been created during this interval—the Pasadena Redevelopment Agency—which was a semi-autonomous agency with powers to acquire land and condemn properties. The PRA took on to itself the chamber's policy of transforming downtown into a modern, densely utilized, high-rise business area.

Gradually protests arose from neighborhood associations and minority groups whose interests were being threatened or neglected by the wholesale development schemes. The struggle came to a head as the PRA pressed ahead with a new burst of high-rise development that would over-shadow the famous and beautiful city hall.

All Saints Church felt that with its downtown location across the street from city hall, it had a moral responsibility to think for the whole community, the poor and the wealthy, the residents and the business people, and to take a position. An ad hoc committee was formed to investigate the issue and recommend to the church what the position should be. John, who was then junior warden at All Saints, was named chair of this committee and commissioned to delve into the matter.

This committee went to work, calling on PRA officials and executives of business corporations as well as meeting with groups of the protesting individuals and organizations. They also studied the city planning phase. As usual, in such matters, each side could advance powerful arguments to justify its position. The committee listened carefully and at the end of an intensive two weeks of work came to the conclusion that the Pasadena Redevelopment Agency was adopting sweeping plans without giving time for the citizenry to be heard, as required by the city charter. The committee recommended to the vestry that the city board of directors be urged to slow down the process of development until the proper citizen input could be given.

Although the vestry was itself divided between rapid development and moderate development advocates, nevertheless it gave unanimous support to the recommended position because of the thoroughness and integrity of the committee's procedures. Thus All Saints was one of the first voices of reasoned restraint to reach the city government in a turbulent period and it forecast a more moderate approach to growth on the part of the city in the future.

Soon afterward, in January 1981, a small group of concerned citizens, feeling the need to carry forward the process of reëvaluation of the community's goals, sought to create a means whereby these could be established in an orderly manner.

William Bogaard initiated the first few informal sessions and John Wood was one of this group, as was Nico Rodriguez, John's colleague in the skills center project. At Nico's initiative they asked John to chair this new venture.

They began by reviving a community enterprise that had been in place a decade earlier. At that time a Goals Congress—which was part of a citizen participation process mandated for the formulation and revision of the city's general plan—was held in Pasadena for the purpose of exploring issues affecting the city and its future. It was to have been a one-time event.

Now, in the view of this group, a new Goals Congress would furnish a more permanent initiative which was needed to redefine the city's future and bring the current issues clearly to the attention of the civic leaders. They felt a need of carefully collecting convictions and presenting them before the city council so that their decisions would be informed, balanced and just for all segments of the community. To start, they got in touch with a score of organizations representing the varying concerns of Pasadena citizens and set about gaining their participation and support.

On May 5, 1981, the *Star-News* carried an article under the heading: "Grass Roots Congress to Probe Pasadena:"

> It is not exactly a vigilante movement, but a group of private citizens and organizations are determined that the grass roots are going to shape Pasadena's future. Pasadena city directors approved the idea Tuesday, endorsing what spokesman John C. Wood termed a Goals Congress for the 1980s that will learn from the public: "What about Pasadena do you want to change?"
>
> "Information and concerns gleaned from the public over a period of months will be translated into objectives and then presented to the city for implementation through various commissions, committees and boards," Wood said. "And then the Goals Congress will monitor the implementation process."

The article concluded by listing a score of organizations, ranging from the Council of Churches to the Junior League and from the Chamber of Commerce to the NAACP who were supporting the Goals Congress, agreeing to participate.

During 1981 and 1982 the congress held meetings and workshops in which nearly 50 organizations of all kinds participated. Emotional issues such as city finances, low- and medium-income housing and a newly proposed downtown urban development plan were aired and debated. In addition the city government made the congress a partner in devising an opinion poll of Pasadena's people on many questions of public import as a basis for shaping city legislation and policies.

John Wood's role in the Goals Congress was summed by Michael Houlemard, one of his fellow members on the skills center task force: "There are so many divergent views in Pasadena, and even though John seems always to be in the eye of the storm, he manages to remain calm in all that confusion. Coalitions change from issue to issue. John always seems to be holding a very firm middle ground, getting the issues clearly out on the table and discussing them. His work in the Goals Congress was a classic example of that. Taking on the Goals Congress in a town of such strong opinions was an extraordinary job—for me an impossible job!"

Looking back on the Goals Congress experience, John says, "What I valued the most was meeting week by week in the evening with that small steering committee group of creative people—Jim Gruettner of ARCO, Karen Cutts, an attorney, Nico Rodriguez of *El Centro*, Pat Dawe, a city planner, and others. It was our job to think and talk together and conceive what could be done.

"It is amazing how much we accomplished, considering our limited hours. Yet what we envisaged of listening to a city in such a way as to help its governing went even beyond what our time and resources enabled. We were perhaps perceiving, but not fully knowing, how to carry out some of the things that my wife, Denise, was later able to take up—listening to people one-on-one and developing the personal links needed to get groups and organizations working together in a deeper way. But we pioneered good things for the city."

During his activities in these civic enterprises, John Wood came to know a couple who led Denise and him into the heart of Pasadena's most painful territory, the Northwest. Now he and Denise were plunged into a section of the city where life was much harder for people. It was an experience which would equip both of them to understand and draw together citizens of very different cultures.

The Reverend John Perkins is a Black crusader, known nationwide for his pioneering work in Mississippi in establishing community centers where along with creating a spirit of reconciliation between classes and races, he has developed health clinics, schools and co-operative enterprises as well. Years before when his brother had been killed by a sheriff, he had fled temporarily from Mississippi to California. Now he and his wife, Vera Mae, exhausted by the demands of their work, came west again to Southern California in 1980 to rest, write and retire.

The Perkins's were lent a home in an affluent district, but after eight months they decided on a bold move. Having learned a good deal about the Northwest area of Pasadena—its reputation as the poorest, most crime ridden, drug infested part of the city—and after touring the neighborhood, they bought a house on a block which was a center of drug trafficking. The local drug boss lived in a house two doors away. The grandson of the old woman who sold them the house was also a drug pusher, and after they moved in, the police raided the house several times, looking for him. Across the street was a house known in the area as "the supermarket," where any kind of narcotic could be purchased.

"We started in," says John Perkins, "to gather together some of the neighborhood kids to play and have a good time. Then we began some prayer meetings and before long we were holding outdoor rallies and bringing a new community spirit into the place.

Perkins was invited to speak at a forum one Sunday at All Saints Church. After the meeting John and Denise introduced themselves and invited him to lunch. Perkins assumed they were going to a restaurant and was surprised when they took him to their home for the meal.

"At the time," he says, "I thought they were rather sophisticated and didn't have much time for poor people and were giving me lunch because I was somebody well known. But quickly we became friends."

By this time, the Perkins' work in the neighborhood had grown to the point where they felt they needed to get it officially organized and incorporated. They named it the Harambee Christian Family Center—Harambee means "Let's get together and push" in Swahili. Perkins invited John to serve on the board and then at the first meeting Perkins asked John to chair the board.

It wasn't long before the drug pushers, feeling threatened, started using violence to oppose what the Harambee Center was doing. "One night," says Perkins, "they knocked out all our windows with bricks and then did it again another night. Twice they firebombed the house—which at least proved we were having an effect on our neighbors.

"At this point police detectives came out and starting living in our house, staking out the place next door. After ten-days surveillance they knew the pattern of our neighbors' moves and early one morning moved in and cleaned up the house, arresting everybody and taking them off to jail—the kids, everybody. All of us were out in the yard, feeling glad about breaking up the drugs, but sad because these folks had become our neighbors. We were all crying.

"Then, one night, the young mother was let out of jail during the pretrial period. She came through our gate asking for 'Grandma Perkins,' as they all called Vera Mae. 'They're going to take my babies away from me,' she said. 'Would you take them and take care of them for me?' My wife assured her that of course we would."

"On the way to court to agree officially to this request, my wife said to her, 'Don't you know that your husband was so violent against what we were doing? Won't he be angry about us looking after your kids?' The mother shook her head and said, 'He's the one who told me to get you guys to take care of them!'

"We were their worst enemy, but they were able to see we were not really their enemy."

The serious nature of this opposition to the Perkinses' work was emphasized in a report on the firebombing by the *Star-News*:

> Police Chief Robert McGowan said the question is whether the bombings were intended to frighten the Perkinses or burn down the center. But he said there is no question the house next door . . . ranks as a prime location for curbside drug dealing where pushers "boldly and brazenly" sell marijuana, cocaine and other drugs. He links the city's 64 percent increase in robberies this year to the drug traffic. He said the offenders usually are young people between the ages of 15 and 25 who are heavily involved in narcotics. . . .
>
> "These young people don't see themselves as criminals but as business people who have a right to control the community," says Perkins, who knows the local drug dealers because they stop by his center to buy sodas from a machine there. "They don't see themselves as particularly mean or unfriendly. Most of them can make $200, $300 or $500 a day by selling drugs. They don't see that as being wicked."
>
> Perkins said their zeal to spread drugs and destruction is "evangelistic," and they probably see him and his work as a stumbling block . . .
>
> Firebombs notwithstanding, Perkins is moving ahead to buy the house on the other side of the one notorious for drug dealings. It will be a "disciples' house" for young black men.

Some time later, Perkins was asked if he had not been taking a risk in asking John Wood to chair the predominantly Black organization. "Yes," Perkins agreed. "Of course, but by then I knew the Woods. John is the kind of person who believes deeply, is honest and open. He does strike you as a little refined when you first meet him, with his Boston accent and all. Besides, John and I have had our disagreements, but I'm someone who comes right out and says what is on my mind when I do. John doesn't fly off, but deals with our differences very creatively. He has been a hard working chair of this committee for three years and he really helped develop the Center."

Perkins' eyes light up as he talks about what has happened in the neighborhood. "A long time back we saw that we needed to focus on the kids. We turned the house next door into a youth place to hold Bible classes, cooking classes and classes for typing, computers, photography, bicycle repair, a little carpentry—in fact, a little skills center.

"Our aim has been to expose the young people to some basic skills—enough so that they can discover things that they like to do. Then we can use that as a basis for motivation, and as a basis for discipline. Most of these kids come from homes and families where there is not much internal discipline—with no father in so many of the homes."

Perkins responds to a question about their long-term goals: He and Vera Mae are seeing other communities start to adopt their methods. The heart of their work is to pioneer the return of the "neighborhood" to neighborhoods.

"We are living as neighbors again—doing things together, borrowing things—and returning them! Other communities are beginning to adopt this way of life. Two young men who served on our board have now started a similar ministry in their area. There is a church very near here, close by the Kings Manor Apartment complex (a low-income housing development with a reputation for being a high-crime area), which is starting to apply our method to that difficult, very poor area.

"We are encouraging 'spin-offs' from this neighborhood—the school we started here has a spin-off into another school. And we have a shelter for the homeless which also has a spin-off in another neighborhood.

"Most of all, we want to create joy again in the community, in the family. That's what society has lost. Some 100 years back a French writer visiting this country described America as great because Americans loved and cared. America was great because it was a country made up of little clusters of community. That is disappearing with urbanization. It's my hope to see the return of community."

Vera Mae, large, motherly, with a big smile, broke into the conversation: "We're big on life and the Lord, here in this corner. What we are doing here is showing the community that there's a better way of life. And we're grateful for all the folks who've been helping us. We never could have gone as far as we've gone without their help—John Crowley, the mayor,

Loretta Glickman, on the city council, and many others. And we're especially grateful to John and Denise. John came out to those board meetings while those drug people were making things difficult on this corner."

Perkins adds, "John and Denise have helped me to be a better person. I came out of Mississippi, lived there during the years of racial conflict. We assumed that the white people who were our opposition in the civil rights movement were in fact our enemy. When conflict came, we dealt with it with power, and many times with confrontation. John and Denise helped me with conflict resolution—to deal with conflict, not from a power base, but on a basis of relationships—relations with those with whom problems must be resolved."

Perkins experienced a dramatic example of the value of such dialogue early on in his friendship with the Woods. Once when the city directors decided to hold a regular meeting in the Northwest instead of in city hall, the usual 15 minutes allotted to questions from the public at the start of the meeting lasted two and a half hours as complaints poured out from local residents.

After this meeting John Perkins was upset at what he felt was the lack of awareness by the civic leaders of the conditions in the Northwest. He chanced to encounter the Woods and announced to them his intention of gathering leaders of the Black community and holding a public meeting at city hall in order to educate the board.

The Woods asked John Perkins whether he had talked personally with any of the directors. When they learned he had not, they suggested he go and see a couple of the most responsible and have a meeting of minds. If that didn't work he could always carry out his plan for a public meeting at city hall.

Perkins decided to adopt this course and instead of precipitating a public confrontation, he laid a basis of communication which set the tone for future frank dealings with the board of directors.

The two couples—John and Vera Mae Perkins and John and Denise Wood—acquired a deep friendship and trust with one another. John Wood's three years as chair of the Harambee Center Board created a lasting bond. To some people the needs in the Northwest sometimes seem insoluble, but not so to the Perkinses and their staff at the center. Neither threats nor painful realities have dislodged them. By their work and their presence they have brought hope into their neighborhood, a hope that is essential to building renewal.

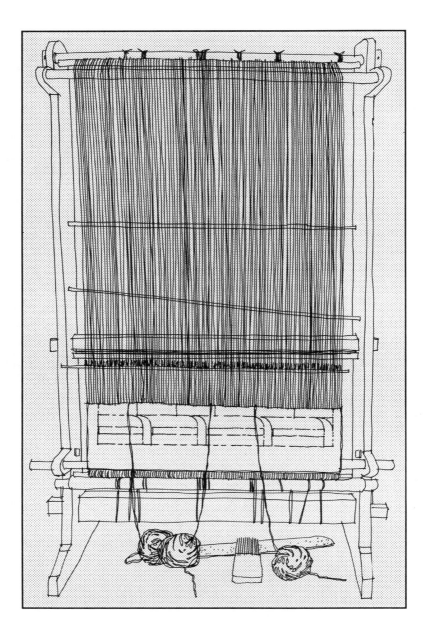

5

Listening to a City

In the process of tackling its problems, the city of Pasadena has an important asset in its community for there are an abundance of professionals, volunteers, agencies and associations committed to improving the quality of life of its citizens. These various sectors rarely coordinated their efforts, however, which diminished their effectiveness.

Beginning in 1983, a recognition grew that the very serious problems facing the city—such as drug trafficking and addiction, crime, inadequate health and child care—needed to be addressed in a much more comprehensive manner. One of those most active in creating the necessary teamwork for this community mobilization of Pasadena's human resources was Denise Wood.

During John's work in the community, Denise was actively by his side, not only supporting him, but launching out into undertakings which paralleled his and strengthened them. An article in the *Star-News* on October 13, 1986, describes their teamwork in the city:

John and Denise Wood are known for their abilities to bring people together. The Woods' bespectacled faces—beaming with an energy that defies their thatches of gray hair—have become familiar to people of all walks of life across Pasadena. As chairman of the City's Centennial Committee, John, 69, worked with all segments of the community. As Director of the Office for Creative Connections at All Saints Episcopal Church, Denise 68, works full time to improve the quality of life among Pasadena's diverse population.

With their aristocratic bearing and refined Eastern accents, the Woods seem a somewhat unlikely pair to be at home in the poverty pockets of town. But building bridges between different races, nations and political groups always has been in their blood. . . . Neither married nor thought seriously of marriage until they were about 50. After they married in 1967 they lived in New York where Denise headed a reading program in Hell's Kitchen and John was frequently on the road with the youth musical production, "Up With People."

They decided it was time to put down roots and buy a home after they moved to Pasadena when John became director of development for the Braille Institute. "It's the first home we ever owned," said John with the relish of a newlywed. They furnished their home in the Linda Vista area with family pieces including a treasured portrait of George Washington, commissioned by John's great-grandfather Lewis Cass, then United States ambassador to France.

"Our only regret is that we waited too long to have children," Denise said. Yet their unpretentious home bespeaks a love of children. There's a bulletin board full of photos of friends' children in their kitchen and Denise has devoted her work in California to children. She was dean of students at Marlborough School in Los Angeles until 1982 and while she and John were co-chairs of All Saints' own centennial in 1983, she produced an in-depth study of Pasadena. . . . In the book she asserts, "The quality of life of all Pasadena's young people must command our highest concern." . . .

Raised by a conservative, proper Bostonian father and stylish Parisian mother who taught French at Wellesley College, Denise appreciates differences. "I began to listen and test climates when I was very young," she said, and sensed the pain that preceded her parents' divorce when she was in her teens. It produced an ability to listen, to put herself in other people's shoes and not pass judgment.

John's father, an Episcopalian clergyman and World War I chaplain, had a big impact on him. "He had the courage to go against the tides of his day. He started me on the long road of learning to honor God and people," John said. He also recalls long summers at the family homestead in Ipswich, Mass., peopled by famous relatives, such as Pulitzer-winning author Louis Bromfield. . . .

People who know the Woods marvel at their relationship. Pat Bond, executive director of the Centennial Committee, recalls when Denise's book was published, John rushed into her office, eagerly waving a copy. "There is a mutual respect and support that probably comes from maturity," she says.

The Rev. Denis O'Pray, associate rector at All Saints, said, "The Woods have what I call a transparency. They do their work. They have their presence. But they don't get in your way. To be with John and Denise Wood is to feel good about yourself."

Denise Wood's career, and particularly her years in Pasadena, was not the result of careful planning, any more than were the achievements of her husband. They were both very conscious that whatever they accomplished in and for Pasadena was the outcome of the organic growth of friendships developed with many people. Her latest project that opened up for her in May 1983 was the result of just such a friendship—one with Don and Lorna Miller.

Don is associate professor of social ethics at the University of Southern California's School of Religion. When John and Don were serving on the vestry at All Saints Church, the idea emerged of the church making a major contribution to the city to mark the centennial of All Saints.

"I remember how Don came up with his idea of listening to people one-on-one," John recollects. "Don had been reading Robert Coles—the Pulitzer prize winner and noted Harvard child psychiatrist—and was impressed by his method of listening to what children were basically saying. Don thought, if we at All Saints Church are going to make a gift to the city, we first of all have to know what people in the city are thinking, what they define as their needs—rather than our church imposing our ideas of our ministry on them.

"The next question was how to figure out who would undertake to find out what people were thinking. Don had the idea that Denise was the one. The idea came out of the blue, but it seemed irrefutable. The next task was simply to convince Denise!"

John recalls, "Denise had by this time been retired from Marlborough School for almost a year. During this period she had been engaged in two fairly major undertakings—the English translation from the French of the book by the Russian dissident, Vladimir Bukovsky, *To Choose Freedom*, and the creation of a documentary film about an unusual French woman, Irene Laure, a leader in the French Resistance during the Second World War and later secretary-general of the 3,000,000 socialist women of France.

"Having finished the taping, Denise was flying home from Paris on a Saturday. I went to meet her at the airport and suddenly as we drove home I heard her saying, 'You know, I think I am ready to go to work again.' I replied, 'That's good, because Don has an idea for you and we have a breakfast date with him on Monday!' "

All Saints Episcopal Church, with its handsome granite buildings and welcoming green lawn, stands across the street from the stately city hall, one of Pasadena's principal landmarks. The church under the leadership of its dynamic rector, George Regas, is known for its active involvement in issues of peace, social justice, women's ordination and other wide-ranging concerns.

In June of 1983, Regas formalized Don Miller's idea and asked Denise Wood to take nine months to research the quality of life of Pasadena and to write a report on her findings as All Saints' centennial "Gift to the City." Regas made no suggestions as to how the work should be done, leaving that up to Denise.

Perhaps because Denise was a lifelong educator, she chose two avenues of approach. One was obvious—to study material already in existence relating to the city—and so she became a familiar figure in city hall.

The second was more original for she chose to interview a wide variety of people, always one-on-one and by appointment, to ask them their perceptions of what it was like to live in Pasadena. With her tape recorder or notebook in hand, Denise tried to go with no hidden agenda of her own which she was trying to prove, but with an open mind and a desire truly to listen to what the other person wanted to say.

Those whom she interviewed often would keep her twice as long as the scheduled appointment; frequently they urged her to go and see so-and-so. Denise took their advice and day after day continued her journey through every part of the city, talking with people of the most diverse backgrounds—a process she called "grazing."

Every Thursday at an early hour and a half breakfast in an office at the church, Denise had the privilege of meeting with three creative, unusual people who had generously agreed to become partners with her in this project—Lou Fleming, a gifted writer of editorials for the *Los Angeles Times* and formerly the head of the *Times'* Rome bureau; her friend Don Miller; and Denis O'Pray, a dynamic young cleric newly arrived on the staff of All Saints Church.

Together this quartet reviewed what Denise had learned during the previous week and talked over what she should do next. Denise admits she was conscious that the three were busy individuals and it forced her to capsulate what she had heard. But their intense interest in what she was reporting kept her energies from flagging and her sense of hope alive.

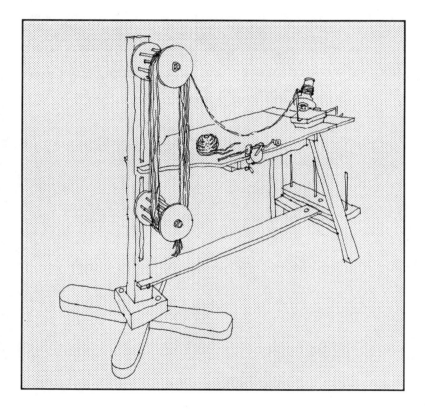

6

Revealing a City to Itself

When George Regas first commissioned Denise on behalf of the church to start this research project, he said he expected her to summarize her work in a report. The deadline for submitting this report was coming up in February 1984. By then she had interviewed more than 100 people and had a stack of notes and tapes. With the help of her three counselors, Denise went urgently to work and completed the report in time to present it to a meeting of the church vestry.

As the four were finalizing the report, the thought crystallized in their minds that there was an urgent need to continue Denise's work. For O'Pray the commitment was to answer polarization in Pasadena, but for Denise the imperative was to face the needs of its children.

Once while Denise was driving with Miller and O'Pray down Orange Grove Avenue wondering together just what shape that continuing commitment should take, into Don Miller's mind came the thought, "creative connections."

"I realized," he said later, "that what Denise was doing was much more than listening to people. In the course of that listening she discovered that a lot of people in the city did not know that others were thinking similar thoughts. So part of her role was as a kind of gadfly to connect people informally."

And so it came about that Denise incorporated into the final section of her report to the church's vestry the proposal that they create "an Office for Creative Connections" to continue the work of research, but also to draw together the many individuals and agencies she was finding who wanted to improve the quality of life of Pasadena.

When she had finished presenting her report to the vestry, they not only gave her a standing ovation, but enthusiastically approved her proposal. So the Office for Creative Connections came into being with Denise named its first director. The vestry also underwrote the budget, providing salaries for a director and a part-time assistant along with office space and services. Five years later Denise looked back at this time and said, "It is wonderful the way that this church sent us out freely into the community, waiting to see what would be the fruit of this effort, making no demands that the work fit a certain pattern."

Published in book form under the title, *Experiencing Pasadena: The Needs, Problems and Tasks of an American City*, Denise's finalized report revealed Pasadena as "a community in pain," as well as being the City of Roses. Poverty, hunger, homelessness, family violence, unemployment and substandard housing were powerful realities which Denise documented with anecdotes and statistics.

Through it all Denise described what she called the "green shoots of hope"—activities where the quality of care, leadership and commitment, much more than the dollars spent, made a crucial difference in bringing hope into people's lives.

There were a wide range of resources already active and vital to the city which Denise described, followed by two specific suggestions in the section, "This We Must Do," where she focused on two imperatives she felt were crucial to the well-being of the city: 1) Pasadena must not be allowed to be a polarized city—one part poor and one part affluent; and 2) the quality of life of all of Pasadena's young people must command the highest concern.

Denise concluded *Experiencing Pasadena* by making clear the ongoing commitment of the Office for Creative Connections which would have four major functions:

1) To *listen* one-on-one in order to keep aware of people's current concerns and perceptions;
2) To *connect* individuals and groups who, by better understanding each other's ideas and aspirations, could make a vital difference in the resolution of the city's problems;
3) To *speak out* on current issues related to the two imperatives outlined in the report; and
4) *To act* by bringing into being from time to time programs or enterprises to improve the quality of life of the city. The Office for Creative

Connections would operate in conjunction with many individuals and institutions who were already active and showing their concern for the quality of life of Pasadena.

Publication of this book catapulted Denise into public life for it was widely circulated. Soon she was in demand as a speaker and her advice was sought by an increasing number of organizations and individuals.

Mayor William Bogaard invited her to appear on his TV program, "Spotlight on City Hall"—the first guest who was not a city hall person. When he phoned to invite her, Bogaard said, "I want you because you think for the whole city."

Another evaluation of the book was made by Nora Mitsumori, head of the Commission on the Status of Women: "You are saying what we are thinking. If we said it, it would be perceived as politics. You are clearly not political, so people listen to what you have to say."

Wilbur Johnson, former head of the Interministerial Alliance, commented: "You are not blaming, no name calling, but you do not water down the truth."

Copies of the book were bought by the Pasadena Library for all its branches and were used as resource material by many social agencies including the Red Cross, World Vision and the Pasadena Junior League. Individual workers spoke to Denise again and again about how useful this text was to them. The Strategic Planning Task Force, which numbered some 160 volunteers from many walks of life who worked together for 18 months to picture what Pasadena should be like in the year 2000, found *Experiencing Pasadena* in the packet welcoming each participant.

An unusual use to which the book was put occurred at city hall where one of the city directors took it apart and pinned its pages to the wall as the board met to plan for the upcoming 15 years ahead. Mayor Bogaard also had Denise speak to his "kitchen cabinet," and the chief administrator of the city invited her to address a breakfast meeting of department heads.

Contemplating the enthusiastic response from many of her audiences, Denise says, "It revealed to me the vacuum in the city about this kind of thinking." Her colleague Denis O'Pray commented, "You are revealing the city to itself."

During the months from September 1983 through January 1984 when Denise was meeting with various members of the community and covering a wide range of topics, Denise was also revealing the city to herself and in the process receiving an education unlike any either Vassar or her previous years had given her. Day after day she was allowing her heart to become vulnerable to what life was truly like for others.

From one interview with the director of an emergency service center she heard of the hard facts of middle-class families, newly unemployed, whose benefits were running out and where domestic violence erupted due to stress from joblessness. She was told heartrending stories of how poor families eked out an existence from one source or another. Many of the stories revolved around single women and their children and Denise began to understand more deeply what was meant by the phrase currently in use, "the feminization of poverty."

Sitting in a windowless, cluttered office, the director mentioned, almost in passing, that since starting to work in this emergency service center, her own T.B. tests had changed from negative to positive.

Another interview led Denise to the special assistant to the president of one of the corporate giants of Pasadena where she heard of the competing claims of business development and cultural considerations. In an effort to maintain a quality of life and control the bulldozing of low-income housing to build high-rise office structures, the citizens had voted for regulations which some companies felt were preventing their future growth.

Since business taxes were the largest section of the city's revenue, the city staff felt the need to take into account conflicting community voices in order to maintain a balance between the two views. Following this debate gave Denise an understanding of how Pasadena could become polarized between rich and poor.

Denise attended an open retreat of city directors held at the Jackie Robinson Center in the Northwest and listened to their discussions which moved restlessly from subject to subject—how to provide basic jobs, how to revitalize the impoverished Northwest area which had the highest unemployment rates and the lowest average income in the city, how to improve the school system, how to find money for repairing curbs and resurfacing streets, how to broaden the tax base, how to attract light industry?

Competing ideas and smoldering tensions made it difficult to reach consensus. Some of the problems the city directors faced were Pasadena born, some came from living adjacent to Los Angeles, others for being in southern California which was going through throes brought on by rapid population growth. The city directors were ordinary, resourceful people who received only the smallest token pay for their services, yet they were at the mercy of constant public scrutiny, as they had to come to grips with intricate issues.

Denise left this gathering wondering how a broader base of community responsibility could be rallied to carry such a heavy weight of needs. Sticking tenaciously to her method of paying individuals the undivided attention she felt they deserved, she approached a woman she had been told she should meet who had a formidable reputation.

Melva Newman is a highly experienced social worker with a great deal of energy which she devotes to her own practice and to helping low-income people. She is best known for her Positive Parenting Workshop at the Jackie Robinson Center.

Denise describes their first meeting—which was typical of how generous people in the community were to welcome her into their midst when she reached out to them. It was also this willingness to befriend and to be a friend which were crucial in building a network of trust and information.

"Melva was trained as a psychological social worker, with a master's degree from the University of Southern California. I phoned her and mentioned a mutual friend who had suggested I get in touch with her because I was writing about the quality of life in Pasadena. She didn't know me and could probably tell from my voice that I was white, yet when I suggested we might meet at a restaurant—thinking that would be neutral territory—she hesitated, then said, 'No, why don't you come to my house? Come and have lunch.'

"When I rang her door bell it was answered by a woman who was helping her around the house and she ushered me into the living room. In the background I could hear a woman's deep voice on the telephone. I looked around the stylish room with a baby grand piano and modern art on the walls. Beyond I saw a dining room table set for two with crystal glasses for water and wine. I was amazed. She didn't know me, but had prepared a marvelous welcome.

"The voice ceased. I turned around. Melva was standing tall and statuesque. She looked me over in silence with a very intensive stare, then came over to me and flung her arms around me. My French half fortunately dominates my Bostonian side, so I could respond with Latin warmth and hugged her back. We moved into the dining room and the lady waited on us, serving a delicious fish meal with white wine. We started talking. Instinctively I felt I should not use my tape recorder and turned it off."

Their conversation, says Denise, ranged over their lives and experiences. The telephone rang and Melva said, "That must be one of my boys," excusing herself.

Her strong voice carried and Denise heard her say, "Yes. You're in jail. That's why you're calling . . . I

74

will tell you what I want you to do. When they let you out on bail, get yourself a job. Earn enough money to pay back what you stole. That's called restitution. If you do it, you'll feel better about yourself. If you don't, you'll never feel good."

Then she hung up and came back. Denise watched this straight-forward, no-nonsense person return. They went on talking and Denise told about her literacy work years before in New York's Hell's Kitchen and her later position as an administrator at Marlborough School in Los Angeles—very different, yet alike.

The two immediately established a bond of shared concerns. Melva told her that every Wednesday evening she ran something at the Jackie Robinson Center for men and women who had their children taken away from them by the court because they had mistreated them or were terrible parents. One of the conditions for getting their children back was to take Melva's course for eight weeks. She invited Denise to attend these sessions and Denise asked if she could bring John.

When Denise and John turned up they found some 35 people—Black, Hispanic and white—quietly sitting around a large room, waiting. Melva swept in and broke the tension, "What can I do to help you? she asked. "Let's gather around and have our time of 'show and tell.' "

A woman spoke up: "This has been a wonderful week. I got my child back from the courts."

The whole room burst into applause. Then Melva said, "I'm going to do a little teaching. Harriet, come on over here please. Take that folding chair and hold it over your head. I want you to walk around. That chair is your problem. I want you all to make a distinction. That chair is not Harriet. Your problems are not you. Most of us feel the weight of that chair and we go lower and lower and dig a hole and bury ourselves in it and the chair is on top of us because we haven't got it clear that the problems are not us."

Then Melva proceeded to the regular part of the evening in which one person could choose to be "in the center." That person's needs would then be addressed by the whole group and all would learn from it. Bill, a Black man in his mid-20s came forward with his wife and a tiny baby and sat together.

"I need help," he said. "I have such anger and hatred against my father. I'm afraid I'll kill him. He's been married five times and my mother was his fifth wife and he mistreated her so badly I hate him. When my wife and I went to visit him he wouldn't let her in the house."

Melva listened and said, "Let's look around the room and see if there's anyone here who reminds you of your father, and we'll do some role playing." Bill's eyes lighted on John Wood. "That man looks like my father!"

John was asked if he would play the role and he agreed. "Just sit opposite Bill," Melva instructed. "Your knees can touch. Maintain eye contact with each other and whatever Bill says, you must reply, 'Yes, my son, I hear you, I believe you'."

Bill's hatred came pouring out, rooted in incident after incident. Finally Melva asked each one in the room to look Bill in the eye and say to him, "You are worthy of love and respect."

When they had finished, a silence fell. Bill's turn was over. Then a young Black woman sitting next to Denise asked Melva for help. "I've got two young children. My boy friend is trying to force me to sell drugs. He says he'll kill me or the children if I don't do it. What should I do?"

Melva replied, "What you need is a police injunction."

"What's that? How do I get it?"

"You go to the police station and pay ten dollars."

"I don't have ten dollars."

"I have," replied Melva, and gave it to her from her purse.

The final event of the evening was ice cream and cake to celebrate someone's birthday in the group. Then it was time to go.

Denise and John were silent as they drove home. This new friendship with Melva had opened up to them both an insight into a part of Pasadena's life which normally they never would have had. That small gathering of people with whom they had sat all evening in that crowded room undoubtedly represented hundreds more like them.

They recognized there was no quick fix to their problems. Dollars alone would not do what was needed for them. Yet the healing, compassion and faith occurring there were remarkable for they instinctively recognized that Melva had in fact helped many parents in the room regain some control over their lives, find some hope of getting back their children from the courts.

But it was clear that forces beyond their control were affecting these people's lives as well. Where would help come from to meet those needs? With only one existing low-cost health clinic operating for two hours each week, how would low-income families find affordable health care? Would vulnerable individuals be overcome by the ruthless ways of the drug pushers?

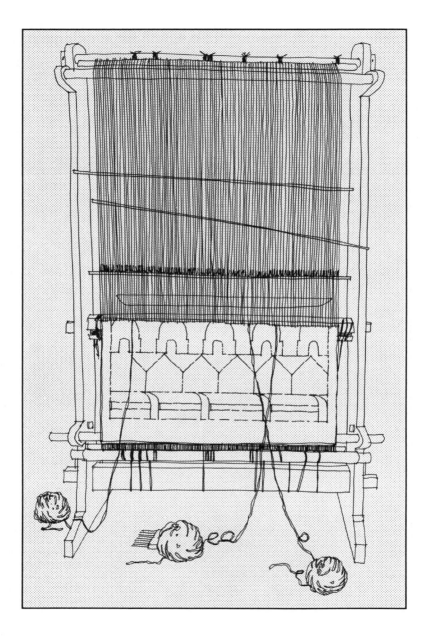

7

Primary Tools: Hard Work and Hope

When the new Office for Creative Connections came into being it had to determine which of the two tough issues raised by *Experiencing Pasadena* would absorb its energies. The obvious concerns were:

1) Pasadena must work assiduously not to be a city polarized between rich and poor; and
2) The well-being of all the community's children must concern everyone.

At an early meeting of the committee members in 1984 Denise invited proposals from the diverse cross-section of people who had gathered. As was to be expected, she received many conflicting suggestions. Sharon Thralls, who was present for the first time, gives a lively account of what went on and how Denise handled the situation. It proved to be a significant beginning of a new initiative in the community.

A dynamic, articulate woman with a handsome home in the affluent community of San Marino which adjoins Pasadena, Sharon has served as president of the Junior League of Pasadena and been active in social concerns for a number of years. In 1986 she was called to Washington to serve on a government committee advising the Social Security Disability Insurance Trust—which handled $30 billion a year and was having problems.

"I was not a member of All Saints," she says, "but the church setting gave me a sense of security that this was no fly-by-night operation. However, when I sat in that first meeting I was scared by some of the people there—people like Melva Newman, the Black psychologist and social counselor.

"I had never had close contact with other races and at that gathering there were people from many varied backgrounds and from many areas of the city. That was what Denise was able to do through that organization—pull together people who didn't understand each other.

"Denise encouraged everyone to speak up, from their different experiences," she recalls. "And they did. I came away feeling that it had been a difficult meeting, but rewarding. It took us two meetings to come to consensus on our priorities and then it was decided to address concerns affecting children and to look for ways to bring together the professionals presently serving them.

"I suppose we felt more at home with the problems of children" said Sharon, "and, too, that we could achieve something in this area. We divided into groups according to our various interests and set out to reach the appropriate professionals, to discern the urgent problems and to clarify the needs."

Sharon took on the creating of two roundtables— one on sexual abuse of children and one on physical abuse of children. Susan Caldwell, a parishioner of All Saints and an active community volunteer, stepped forward to create the parenting skills roundtable. Lou Fleming's wife, Jean, also an All Saints parishioner and a trustee of Pacific Oaks College known for its teacher training in human development, volunteered to marshal the roundtable on early childhood development.

Conscious of the need to refresh busy professionals, great care went into the planning for these round-tables which were held at All Saints' spacious forum. They were to run from 4:40 to 8:30 p.m. on a weekday. Cool drinks, crackers and cheese awaited the participants (many of them tired from driving on a crowded freeway). Each time 16 professionals sat at a hollow square table to address a carefully worked out agenda which had been mailed to them several days beforehand to help keep the discussion focused on the issue of that day.

At 6:15 the group broke for supper—a tasty, simple meal of soup and salad waiting on the buffet. Everyone could sit where they wished at tables set for eight and frequently people who knew each other professionally ate a meal together for the first time, so once a superior court judge and an emergency room worker found themselves sitting opposite one another.

At 7:00 work resumed and promptly at 8:30 they were dismissed. The evaluation sheets filled out at the end reflected two themes: 1) We met well-known people in our field whom we'd not known before, and 2) You worked us hard but we left reinvigorated.

A few weeks after the last roundtable certain teachers and professionals in the community told Denise and Lorna Miller, who by now had become Denise's associate, "Unless you address the issues of teenage pregnancy, drugs, alcohol and gangs, all the rest will hardly count."

Those four issues were daunting, yet such heartfelt advice had to be followed. Once again the process of making friends, building trust and gaining insight was entered into. The church agreed to continue supporting Denise and Lorna, through this next phase, both financially and by its nurturing, but it was one the two carried out basically on their own.

Denise worked five days a week, Lorna three. Their method was as before, taking the time needed to meet one-on-one with all sorts of individuals and listen deeply to what each one wanted to say. Quietly their presence and their concern were making themselves felt.

They joined with others in partnership to move child care from being a women's issue to making it a community issue. Bit by bit a few farsighted employers, together with the Commission on the Status of Women, the Commission on Children and Youth, the Child Care Consortium were gaining the ear of the wider community about the urgent need for affordable, accessible and quality child care. Denise's writing and speaking were valuable components of the campaign.

Pasadena Planned Parenthood and the Office for Creative Connections cosponsored a morning workshop dealing with the growing problem of teenage pregnancy. It was decided that rather than having a panel of four or so speakers with a short time for questions from the floor, 14 professionals with hands-on experience with young parents would be asked to speak briefly during the first hour.

The second hour was devoted almost exclusively to questions from the floor addressed to the panel members. Their words carried weight and many were eager to take the discussion further. At one point 16 hands were in the air trying to catch the moderator's eye. A palpable quietness descended on the group as a young girl, resident at a local nonprofit home for teenagers, spoke of her gratitude at being taken in after her parents, learning she was pregnant, evicted her from their home.

Finally Denise rose to sum up the morning, making two points: 1) A heart that has been empty too long is likely to cause a womb to become full too soon; and 2) The best contraceptive is a viable future. The Pasadena *Star-News* reported her second point on the front page and the work of cementing partnerships and raising community awareness went on.

In July 1985 Denise was approached by the corporate headquarters of the Los Angeles United Way—the area's major fund-raising and distributing organization. They were interested in what she was accomplishing in drawing together professionals in the social service field, they said, and were wanting to offer her a grant of $20,000 "to enhance and improve cooperation and communication between agencies serving youth at risk."

This was the first time, it seemed, the United Way had offered to finance a process, rather than a program or a product. Denise accepted the offer and undertook to spend half her time on it, working out a framework for the researching of the resources of the four areas on which the Office for Creative Connections would concentrate: 1) Substance abuse; 2) Teenage pregnancy; 3) Health services for low-income youth and children from birth to age 19; and 4) Training youth in job skills.

The project began in November 1985 and continued until April 1987. It soon became clear to Denise that few in Pasadena had an overview of any of the fields they were studying. Together with Lorna Miller and Francisca Neumann—an experienced substance-abuse professional—they now made up the staff of the Office for Creative Connections.

Their first move was to enlist the help of the central library of Pasadena, which took off their shoulders an impossible amount of paperwork by organizing a data bank in the Public Access Library Services (PALS) on the first three of the priority fields. Unfortunately the Office for Creative Connections did not have the personnel to embark on the fourth issue—training youth in job skills.

After completing some 147 interviews on teenage pregnancy, drugs, alcohol and gangs, faithful to her desire to increase community awareness about children, Denise wrote a second book entitled, *Growing Up in Pasadena: What Are Our Children Telling Us?*

The publishing of this text led to a significant development in her work in the city. Already she had moved from the initial phase of "grazing"—getting to know individuals and organizations who could provide information about the needs of the community and what was being done to meet them—to a second one—making connections between these people and encouraging them to cooperate in important endeavors. Now she realized she was entering a third stage—through the Office for Creative Connections she had the means to mobilize some of these people to form new organizations which would tackle large tasks which had been too formidable to undertake without such close teamwork.

The book was hailed by the Pasadena *Star-News* on June 24, 1987, in an editorial labeled, "Growing Up."

It is all too easy to despair about the world's woes over which individuals seem to have little or no control. The seemingly unending list of problems make it difficult to imagine that solutions to many of the most pressing social problems begin at home.

Denise Wood, the author of two reports on life in Pasadena has zeroed in on as big a chunk of the overall problem as exists under one roof—children. Armed with the cold, hard facts about modern society's most defenseless victims, Wood is confronting head-on the outmoded conventional wisdom with which society approaches so much of what is wrong in the '80s and is struggling mightily to bury the rationalizations by which so many adults choose to ignore what is undeniably a growing cancer threatening the very existence of the family.

Her primary tools for unearthing creative solutions to the underlying causes of gangs, drug abuse, teenage pregnancy, youth crime and joblessness are hard work and hope.

The messages of Wood's new book, *Growing Up in Pasadena*, are a direct offspring of the conclusions of *Experiencing Pasadena*, her first report on the quality of life in the city. Staking children to the self-esteem that spawns a natural belief in a viable future is a potent antidote to loneliness and poverty. Reminding parents that what happens to all children is important to everyone is an eternal verity to which too little energy and too much lip service is too often paid.

Growing Up in Pasadena is a clarion call for mobilization in a time of bewildering fragmentation. Wood's timely exhortation for togetherness is itself part of the solution, for it reminds us all of the universal need to "love thy neighbor." Therein lies the hope of a brighter future for all mankind.

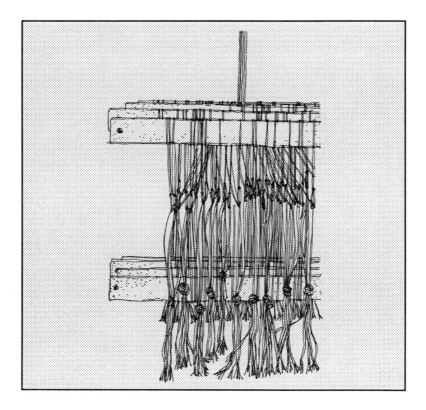

8

Goats, Pizzas and Computers

Early on in her "grazing" process, Denise realized how much there was to learn from each person she met. Having no hidden agenda, but being keen to listen, she found all sorts of insight, wisdom and intuition came out so naturally in the conversations. It did not make problems disappear, but it set up a quality of communication which made it possible to believe that genuine solutions, or progress towards solutions, could come about.

One such conversation took place with Bruce Philpott in the summer of 1985. Bruce had just been loaned by the Pasadena Police Department to the city manager's office to oversee making effective a city master plan for revitalizing the Northwest. This involved dealing with the economic and social needs of the area that underlay the chaos of youth gang wars, drugs and a high juvenile crime rate. Day by day, Bruce set about bringing people together, listening to them and paying attention to those in pain—and in the process bringing a personal element into city government "north of the 210 Freeway"—the needy area of Pasadena.

A tall, forceful person, Bruce's accessibility and practical responses to people won trust from all sides. One day, he telephoned Denise saying that people had told him he should get to know her since she knew a lot about the city. They scheduled a half-hour appointment and he stayed for an hour and a half. Denise liked him and his dedication and felt he was aiming in the right direction.

They began having lunch together every three weeks or so to talk shop about the city. During the winter he said to her one day, "We've tried half a dozen things out of city hall in the Northwest. Four of them have bombed and unless we find out what had made them bomb, there's no point in trying out more."

Denise suggested getting together a few friends with grass roots experience in for a meal. "Fine," said Bruce. "Go ahead and arrange it."

Ten days later they sat down together for breakfast at 6:45—Melva Newman; J.C. Lowery, a young Black activist who was then on the staff of Planned Parenthood; John Perkins of the Harambee Christian Family Center; James Shepherd, a staff member of the YMCA who had previous experience inside gangs and had served time in prison; Lindy DeWit, ebullient, unorthodox director of Girls Club; Denise and Lorna Miller.

At once Bruce Philpott made it open season on his work. Lowery and Shepherd jumped in without hesitation: that school, they said, where you were trying to get something going—the kids hate the principal. That area where you wanted to do something belongs to one of the street gangs. The other gang won't put a foot there. They were very blunt and direct. As he finished this criticism, Lowery peered at a solemn Bruce and said, "Don't take this personally."

It was now 8:45 and Denise thanked everyone for coming and said they'd better let everyone get off to work. Someone interrupted and said, "We must meet again and evolve a strategy."

So they did, the following week with Denise and Lorna providing the breakfast. Quickly the conversation turned to street kids—how desperate they were and at loose ends. They talked about a federal program that paid low-income youth minimum wage for summer employment. In the past local employers each year would state how many of these youngsters they could put to work in their operations over the prescribed eight-week period.

Focusing on the young people's self-esteem or helping them learn to deal with anger or frustration were not necessarily high on these employers' concerns. They had to meet daily work loads and produce. Yet, unbridled resentment and a poor sense of self-worth could ruin the job opportunity and make the chance of a work experience far less productive for both employer and employee than it might have been.

Suddenly, recalls Denise, the suggestion was made: Why don't we develop a pilot summer youth employment program (SYEP) that has as its basic purpose the strengthening of the self-esteem of these young folk? That idea began a series of meetings every other week, month after month which were dubbed, "Breakfast with Bruce." Soon news went out over the grapevine. People came in to help. There was no money, so gifts were proffered in cash and kind.

Perkins lent a van for field trips for kids. Philpott got the use of a city truck plus paint and brushes so they could paint out graffiti. More facilities were offered: the Girls Club of Pasadena, where the youth could be trained in running simple recreational programs for girls; the YMCA where participants could be taught the use of a computer using software related to job skills and then be taken to visit job sites.

A police car wash was set up where they could wash and wax cars and a program was established at the Sage Hill Ranch where they could feed and care for the animals, clear brush and plant vegetables. The SYEP participants also had six group sessions with Melva Newman where they discussed issues related to their lives.

The pilot program was launched on July 4th, 1986, with 16 young men and women participating and which ran for eight weeks. Along the way the decision had been made to enroll young people who were not only unemployed, but had already run afoul of the authorities and were on probation, in remand homes or the like. There were few illusions about the toughness of the assignment among the breakfast group, but they felt that if the program achieved some measure of success with these more difficult cases, it might generate more hope for what many felt to be an insoluble problem. All the adults who joined in making the program work were special people—role models—teaching from the heart out.

The participating ranch was run by a gifted couple, Eugene and Brenda Pickett. To work with the young street kids demanded a great deal of energy on their part. Eugene had his own private security business and had to make time from it to work alongside the young people in the heavy task of brush clearing. Brenda was by inclination and training a singer with four young children to care for plus a part-time job at the Pasadena Central Library. She had the same bluntness and follow-through with the young teenagers as she did with her own children.

These two courageously undertook their assignment, thinking about, caring for and working with these difficult-to-handle young people—a group few were eager to employ. Eleven young people completed the program—two had to be dropped when their behavior became too disruptive, three others quit.

When it was all over the breakfasters held a debriefing session where those responsible for the program agreed that it had been worthwhile, especially in attaining the goal of building self-esteem in the participants—who had arrived unruly, unresponsive and unappreciative. Some remarkable changes in attitude had taken place. A consensus agreed that the ranch, especially, had provided a unique learning opportunity for the trainees who grew by leaps and bounds.

Jon, who lived in a group home, had been a surly teenager when he first arrived at the ranch. Each morning he was given charge of a pony which had been mistreated. It took three weeks for Jon to build minimum trust with the animal. One day a loud crash caused the pony to bolt to the far end of the paddock. Jon was furious. A young woman who worked at the ranch turned and asked him, "Why do you think he ran away?"

Jon shrugged his shoulders, "Scared, I guess."

She probed, "Why do you suppose the pony was scared?"

Jon thought a moment, "Oh, I suppose bad things had happened to him, but he could trust me. I wasn't going to hurt him."

"Jon," she replied, "he'd been beaten for years, and he's only known you for three weeks."

Slowly Jon nodded, "I don't trust anybody either."

Once when a horse was chewing on the wood fence, one of the youth wanted to know why it was doing such an idiotic thing. The ranch hand rejoindered, "When you're bored, what do you do?"

There was no answer so she continued, "Isn't that when you start stealing and getting in trouble?"

Looking sheepish, the young boy allowed it was pretty stupid, and then after a thoughtful moment concluded, "Oh, is that why I do that? I get it!"

A big tough named Fernando, known for his macho attitude, was given an old mare to care for. To everyone's surprise he treated her quietly and with consideration. Without prodding he cut her bangs and would wash and dry her off. The mare was deathly afraid of the saddle, but daily Fernando would patiently work for 15 minutes to get it on her back. Another side to him had been allowed to surface.

Peter was scared to death of horses and loudly proclaimed, "You're not going to get me in that pen." He was convinced the horse would kill him. But the reward for three weeks of good behavior was being allowed to ride. When Peter's good conduct brought him the opportunity, he was told no one was going to push him, but he should learn as much as the others. Finally he managed five minutes on the horse and later that day was heard, proudly showing another kid with a sawhorse, "See, this is what you do."

For some reason the young people were able to let their guard down with animals. They were placed in a non-threatening, non-judgmental situation in which they could examine their own behavior, not having to be defensive or to justify. The farm work itself was demanding and they were pushed to their physical limits.

The first day the group showed up, the young woman in charge of the program showed the group the feed barn where she proceeded to lift a sack of feed on to her shoulder and walk out to the paddock, demonstrating the procedure. Only when the boys tried to lift a sack did they discover how heavy it actually was.

Nearly five weeks into the program one of the most taciturn of the participants who was a real loner showed up unexpectedly one Saturday morning at the near-empty ranch. Mr. and Mrs. Pickett said hello, but didn't ask him what he was about. Accompanying him in his battered jalopy was his mother and the two silently got out and walked up the hill to where the goats were penned—the goats were his special charge during the week. After a while mother and son returned to the car and drove away. The next Saturday morning the same jalopy appeared. This time the lad carried his passenger of the vehicle. His sister, a paraplegic, was thus conveyed up to visit the goats. Obviously his was a heart coming alive.

The following summer the project was repeated and 30 young people signed on for additional funding had been found. The 23 boys and 7 girls, aged 14 to 18, were Black, Hispanic and white. Of these 23 completed the session. The curriculum was similar, but it also included landscaping around the Rose Bowl plus a chance to create theater skits from their own experience. Tutoring in English and math was scheduled as part of the work day, for pay, for those who specially needed it.

Denise describes Melva Newman's expert handling of the youth at one of her weekly sessions. "Melva arrived a couple of minutes late with two boxes of pizza. At the previous session they had collected money to pay for it, but the money was only enough for one pizza. Melva had decided they needed another and when she put them on the table, she pointed to one and said, 'That's the one you all bought. This one is the pizza of Unconditional Love. I want you to understand that idea. In life there is unconditional love—some things are given us which we don't deserve and have no right to.'

"One of the boys got up and said, 'I'm not eating any pizza I haven't paid for,' and went over to a corner, tilted his chair against a wall and pulled his hat over his eyes. No one knew what to do, but finally a young boy took a wedge over on a paper plate and held it in front of his nose. It smelled very good and he finally opened his eyes, came over and ate the pizza. It was amazing to watch the humorous and alive ways Melva used to make an abstract idea like love understandable."

Another session Denise had that second summer was held out under the trees. Melva had a simple procedure: Everyone had to stand up and say two things he or she liked about himself or herself. One of the girls stood and said hesitantly, "I like my hair and my nose."

Immediately there were comments from the boys about her body, but Melva firmly stopped them. "We're not going to have that kind of conversation. We're listening to what Mary thinks about herself. I want each of the boys to look Mary in the eyes and repeat what she said: 'Yes, you have nice hair and a nice nose.' Or you can say anything nice about her you want."

How hard it was for those rough, tough young men to say something to a young woman that was not coarse or obscene. Although they writhed, hit the dust and horsed around, Melva quietly insisted on the process and made them tell one another what they liked about themselves and then had this affirmed by the group.

When they were alone after this session, Denise conjectured to Melva that she supposed with street boys it was always a struggle for power and sexual dominance for there appeared to be no two-way communication with the girls.

Melva agreed emphatically, "Exactly. And as they do these kinds of exercises they learn to prize what is in themselves and experience something of other people's caring." She added, "At the start of the program, I told them they were special. They looked at me as if I was crazy. But now they are beginning to believe me. One of the young men rode a motor bike without a helmet. I kept getting after him about it, and he is beginning to realize that I care about him.

"Early on I made plain my idea about sexuality— about how one needed to postpone having children until one is able to bring them up properly. And at the start the group tried to shock me, so I merely responded and told them they were true poets! They move from impulse to action. We need to work to get them to move from impulse to thought to action. My sadness is it takes more than I can give them. The kids think I can help them, but so much more is needed than we have."

The third summer the Office for Creative Connections sponsored another SYEP pilot project. Like the others it was designed to increase self-esteem as well as give the young people paid employment. That year the program was entirely built around theater. The young people wrote scripts, went out to gather audiences and performed for seniors, very young children and the general community. Eugene and Brenda Pickett once more gave of themselves to be, with others, responsible for twelve young people assigned to them for those hectic summer weeks.

Funding for the adults' salaries had come during these three experimental summers from both private and public sources. World Vision, Avery International and the Moseley Foundation caught the vision of these pilot programs. Some of the city's seed money for innovative initiatives was also granted to the Pilot SYEP through the conduit of "Toward 2000"—a citizen managed group which dispensed city funds.

An idea of the challenge, as well as the effectiveness of the project, was expressed in the official report evaluating the program:

> The staff worked well together and were sensitive to dealing with hard core youth, but need to undergo extensive workshops on coping with the youth of today. Today's young people have to handle the issues of drugs, gangs, AIDS, air and water pollution. The pilot's participants had already experienced brushes with the law and violence in their own homes before they joined the program. Four who voluntarily withdrew themselves ended up in jail before the summer was over.
>
> A program as unusual as this one would not have succeeded without the participation of adults who understood the importance of self-esteem and who had a genuine interest in helping these at-risk youngsters make something of their lives. . . .

The future of this program could be very dynamic. . . . By putting our young people to work and addressing many of their personal needs for education and for a sense of personal worth and responsibility, we help curb the cycle of crime, depression and despair. . . . The basic goal of the program is unique as it focuses on the inward needs of young people as well as the outward ones. A coalition of public and private agencies, a gifted staff of adults are already gathered around this task; their work needs to be continued.

By 1987 the city administration of the regular SYEP program recommended the continued weekly use of the counseling component which the Office for Creative Connections' pilot SYEP had pioneered. One counseling conversation a week was suggested in the procedural handbook for the employers taking part in the program.

Unfortunately sufficient funding was not available to carry out ongoing evaluation of what happened in the lives of the young people who had been a part of each of the summer experience. What was learned unmistakably, however, was the detailed, skillful care needed, in abundant measure, to make any impact on the lives of a generation of very wounded individuals.

Speaking about the needs of street kids in today's Pasadena, Gerda Steele, the executive director of the city's Commission on the Status of Women, expressed it powerfully to Denise, "Our present situation probably did not happen overnight. The lure of money is so powerful, yet it is death money when it is linked to drugs. These kids don't have long to live. They are kamikazes. I know nine- and ten-year-olds who look at you with dead eyes. It's a futureless generation, living for the moment."

Prentice Deadrick directs the Jackie Robinson Community Center in Northwest Pasadena and is also responsible for the spacious, well-lit park across the street. During the summer of 1988 he had been most supportive of Brenda Pickett's theater work with the SYEP young people. For a long time gang activity, drug pushers and low staffing had made residents of the area skittish about using the park, despite the advantages of the clubhouse and excellent gym. Prentice was glad to have upbeat activity going on daily in the clubhouse. Other programs had cooperated with Brenda's and together they had created a healthy attitude of hard work.

Talking with Denise in May 1989, Deadrick commented on how much more the park, clubhouse and gym were now being used. The city had increased the staffing level from one and a half to eight people as a result of community pressure. New all-year programs were now in place. For the moment families and gang members were tacitly respecting each other's need for recreation. A fragile truce, but as Prentice pointed out, every hour that gang members and dealers were not on the streets outside the park was a gain.

Deadrick's words to Denise had a prophetic note, "Among the group in the park there is a lot of wisdom about how our many problems should be tackled. There has to be: these people are so close to the problem. I am trying to empower them, to teach them the language of the dominant culture so that all that intelligence can be made to count. We must keep an ear to the heart of the community."

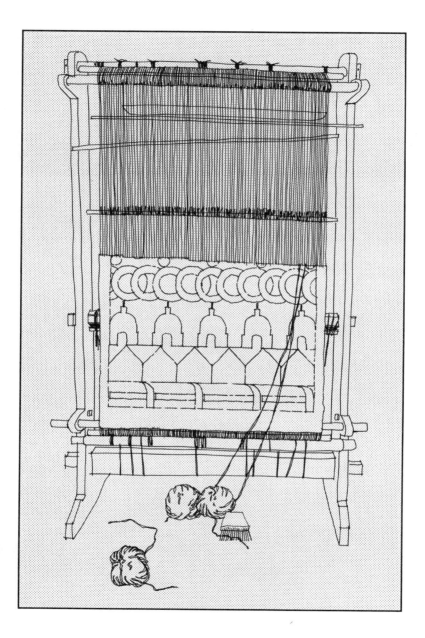

9

Relieving a City of Cynicism

In California there are not many communities that are old enough to celebrate a centennial, but Pasadena is among them. The settlers from the Midwest incorporated their city June 13, 1886. Some two years before the centennial, Mayor William Bogaard and some of his colleagues were giving thought to how best to celebrate the event.

Pasadenans for the past several years had been expressing more vocally their special interests and their divergent views about the future of the city. Bogaard felt keenly that the centennial should be an expression of that diversity, but also be a tool to help portray the unity of the whole community.

In the summer of 1984 the office of the city manager was asked to prepare a report recommending the appointment of a centennial committee, the hiring of an executive director and the budgeting of expenses. In October Bogaard nominated 17 members of the centennial committee from among a number of volunteer applicants who represented all the classes, races and sections of the city.

An extensive search for a paid executive director who would guide the administration of the whole enterprise resulted in selecting Patricia Bond, an able, energetic person with a lot of flair who had proved her ability running election campaigns, especially for minority candidates. Then Bogaard and his colleagues sought a chair to head the centennial committee, finally inviting John Wood to fill the position.

Reflecting on his choice, Bogaard says, "There was a sentiment among the city council to go to a business leader, a pillar of the chamber of commerce. At the same time there was a sentiment that that would be a mistake, rather that we should go to the minority community, to someone Black or Hispanic or of another minority who would ensure that aspect of the city would be featured in any centennial celebration, as it should be. But some of us on the council saw John Wood as a person who represented both of these interests very effectively. He had demonstrated his concern for the ethnic communities and the distinctive neighborhoods and he understood that Pasadena's strength lay in large part in its vital, active, diverse life. He also, although not a member of the business community, had in a relatively short time through his work in the community earned credibility with them."

When Bogaard and John Crowley, the vice mayor, called at the Woods' home and laid the proposition before him, John felt both surprised and honored, but foreseeing that the undertaking would be totally absorbing for the next two years, he declined. They continued to urge him, as did another member of the board, Loretta Thompson-Glickman, who had been Pasadena's first Black mayor.

"Loretta phoned me early one morning," John recalls, "and in her typical manner said, 'What's all this, John, about your not accepting the chair of the centennial committee?' I explained to her, but as I drove to work that morning, I said to myself, 'If people keep knocking at your door, sooner or later you've got to open it. There's something Biblical about that.'

"When I arrived at the office, I phoned Loretta back and told her, 'I'll do it.' I felt that if I could help in any way to bring the city together, it was worth the time and effort. Moreover, my colleagues at Braille Institute said to me, 'This is a marvelous chance to serve your community. You've helped us to grow in these past twelve years. Now we'll back you in whatever time you need to do this centennial job.' "

Loretta maintains, "One of the reasons we wanted John to be chair of that committee was because we knew it was going to be a tough job. We also knew we had a lot of diverse groups that needed to be drawn together and that was going to take a very special kind of personality who wasn't afraid of visibility. And there was one further thing. In picking John Wood we knew we would also be getting two people for we'd also have Denise! We'd have a team that supports one another."

John now found himself, a dozen years after their arrival in Pasadena, in a unique position of responsibility for the uniting the community. All of his experience in reconciling divergent interests and a deepening understanding of distinctive cultures would now be put to fullest use in this civic enterprise.

His first appointment was Loretta herself to serve as vice-chair. One of his next appointments was Bessie Shenk to be corporate secretary. She was known throughout the city for her participation over many years in civic affairs. The three of them and Pat Bond had breakfast together once or twice a week for the next 18 months. From the first, the relationship between John and his executive director, Pat Bond, was crucial.

Looking back on the centennial, Pat jokes, "I think some people chose John Wood as a balance to me. I was regarded as a 'wild Italian,' a liberal Democratic politician. John looked conservative and quiet. I was a little worried, myself. I like to maintain control in what I do! So I didn't know how we would get on. As it turned out, we worked beautifully together, a great match of different personalities!"

"Let me tell you outright," says John, "Pat was the genius of the centennial. Her flare, her courage and her grit made it go. My job was to back her up."

The basic reason for their close teamwork, Pat says, was their agreement on what the centennial should be all about. It was to be really inclusive. That might sound innocuous, but it was not. There was a group which was used to controlling what went on in any volunteer work in Pasadena. For years the city had been pretty well under the influence of the upper class.

So, says Pat Bond, to keep the centennial inclusive was a daily, exhausting proposition—it was like walking through a minefield. "I didn't want to exclude the old guard, any more than the others. Their vision of the centennial, as it turned out, was totally different from mine, but it was important.

"We ended up, after 18 months, with every decision having been made by every class and color—there were power struggles all the way through—but everyone came out of it feeling good about everything."

"A good example of what went on arose from the decision to have a parade to celebrate all the elements of Pasadena's life. The first problem, of course, was that Pasadena already had a famous parade—the Tournament of Roses. The aim of the centennial parade was very different—to portray the diverse heritage of the Pasadena community, but some of those in the parade committee had a different vision. Their first suggestion was to put all the minorities in one red street car, with some slogan such as 'We were happy in the 1900s'!

" 'No,' we said, 'minorities are going to be part of every section of the parade—bands, athletes, old families, and so on. And more than that, they're going to be part of the whole planning of the parade and everything in the centennial.' That meant, of course, that all the upper planning committees had to be integrated. That was a three- or four-hour fight. There were people who thought it would never work—too diverse a group.

"It was an interesting progression. First the power struggle was unspoken, then it came to the surface, and then it was fought out. It was a full-time job to make it an inclusive celebration without people hating each other! The principle was to integrate from the top and let it trickle down. It was hard work, but out of it came a lot of creativity.

"When I saw the parade drive by I was choked up—it was so poignant. It was not the Rose Parade. It was a genuine, beautiful hometown parade, depicting Pasadena's life and history. I found myself thinking, 'I've done more for human understanding, working on this parade, than I'd done in electing people to political office—my life's work.' In that parade John and I had made a social statement—every shape, size, color and class of person united, and in such good feeling."

One of the most formidable tasks was raising the funds for the ambitious program that was planned. John and Pat immediately ran up against a problem in the business community—the main source of revenue.

A lavishly planned Army-Navy football game had been held a few years earlier in the Rose Bowl. It had been a loss financially and a number of business people had been hurt by it and were wary about any further such events. Also, the business community was still unhappy about an increase in their license taxes levied by the city. Clearly, fund-raising was a matter of urgency and also one that called for imagination.

The key to its success was a brilliant occasion held nine months before the date of the centennial. A

"Stroll Through the Decades," held on September 17, 1985, on a square in front of the illuminated city hall, was an elegant dinner, beautifully served for nearly 1400 people, with music and entertainment. Accompanying it was a program listing sponsors and subscribers and their accomplishments through the decades. The event netted $126,000, close to half the funds needed for the centennial celebration. More than that, it set the pace for money raising and staging of events from then on. No one any longer had doubts that "Pasadena could do it."

Centennial Super Week started on June 14, with the centennial parade where 3,500 participants and 107 entries drew an enthusiastic crowd of some 20,000—the first of many events. Volunteers from the Tournament of Roses gave it a touch of class by their handling of the logistics of the parade; participants from Spanish and Mexican heritage, Black, Asian and every community, gave it color and nostalgia and made everyone feel it was their parade.

John Perkins affirmed Pat's feeling about the parade, "For the first time in my life," he said, "I have seen a real people's parade." Nico Rodriguez, the Hispanic attorney concurred, "That parade turned this city around."

The great day itself, June 19, began with an open-air gathering in Garfield Plaza, now renamed Centennial Plaza, in front of the city hall, with a seated audience of more than 2,500 and 8,000 more standing around. Speeches and lively entertainment were enjoyed by all. A citizens' strategic planning program looking to the year 2,000 was announced by

Bill Bogaard and a time capsule for the year 2086 was presented. Church bells rang in unison across the city and 28,000 balloons in centennial colors soared into the summer sky.

The party continued that evening with more festivities and California Attorney General and Pasadena hometown boy, John Van de Kamp, cut an enormous birthday cake whereupon the audience of some 15,000 joined in singing patriotic songs and the extravaganza was broadcast over the Voice of America and telecast by NBC News.

After the centennial celebration was over, a city director asked Pat, "How did you and John manage to integrate the centennial? We've been trying to integrate people for years."

She replied, "There has to be a will. Then you go the extra mile to break through the incidents of fear on each side. Now," she says firmly, "The centennial has become a standard. It showed what was possible. In a sense, it relieved the community of cynicism. How those varied volunteers could work together has become a role model. Pasadenans have begun to change in the way they think about each other."

During this Super Week, the *Star-News* asked John Wood to contribute an article about the meaning of the centennial. After outlining the history of the settlement and early years of Pasadena and a description of centennial highlights to come, he wrote:

> One final thought. I've been reading about the early settlers. I've been reading their letters. They were very human people. They had their needs and

their hardships. They had their hopes. But they also had their determination to do something about the needs and the hopes, and to do it together.

Today we're in the same place, I think. We're at the beginning of our second hundred years. We're also at the beginning of a era in the world, where cities like ours are little global villages in which people from all parts of the world have come to live and work together. Here we are, the Blacks who have endured so much in our country and who have so much to give; the great-hearted people from the Spanish-speaking lands; the vital, industrious boat people and others from Southeast Asia; the Armenians with their memories and energy; the Midwesterners and Easterners who have long roots back to Europe—all of us as Americans, all with needs and hopes. Some of the needs and hopes go deep. It is for us now to have the determination to do something about these needs and hopes, and to do it together.

That is the meaning of the centennial in our eyes—to bring the people of the city together, together to work for a future that will benefit and honor us all.

On the eve of the Fourth of July, the *Star-News* published an editorial under the title, "Special People":

To say that the Fourth of July this year is something special for Pasadena is a gross understatement. Celebrations of Independence Day in the heat of a typically hot Southern California summer usually have little competition. But 1986 is different. This Fourth celebration is a milestone for

the city and its people. It coincides with Pasadena's
100th birthday, and Friday night's circus and fireworks
show at the Rose Bowl concludes the city's official
centennial series of big events. As such, it is time to
shake a few hands for the magnificent job done in
planning the city's birthday. Hundreds of volunteers
deserve residents' gratitude. And they are sure to get
some applause, albeit nameless, during the Pasadena
centennial salute that is planned Friday just before
the fireworks begin.

Two people in particular will be long remembered
for their tireless efforts to make Pasadena's 100th
year a fun and inspirational one. They have kept the
centennial on track through thick and thin. To
Centennial Chairman John Wood and to Centennial
Committee Executive Director Pat Bond, our
heartiest thanks for a job well done.

Asked what she was proudest of about the
centennial, Pat Bond replied, "All the creative energy
we experienced. It brought everybody together—Black,
brown, white, the rich and the poor—everyone felt they
were a part, and they felt good about themselves as
a result." She sums up her working relationship with
John Wood: "He listens, he is interested, he considers.
But he can also be very strong, very tough. He stood
on his principles a couple of times when it was very
difficult to do so. His style is nonconfrontational. He
likes people and that shows through. He's dignified—a
graceful person."

When asked if she feels the uniting process which
was so effective in the centennial is applicable in
wider fields—in the political sphere, for example, with

which she is so familiar, Pat responds, "Well, politics is of course confrontational. But there are politicians who speak to the best in people, as well as others who speak to the worst. I think the country is craving right now for people who speak to the best. People are looking for a dose of altruism, idealism. That was what we did—spoke to the best in people in Pasadena. We held up some lofty goals. And people felt good about themselves."

Bessie Shenk, the centennial corporate secretary, evaluated it from her own angle. Her father was a central figure in Pasadena for much of his life and she grew up with a great interest in civic affairs. "You can't help have some positive fallout from the centennial. Of course there's still plenty of dissension, but many people have changed. I'm convinced that the community moved together. And perhaps the most significant change is that we are beginning to plan *with*, instead of *for* people. And Pasadena is thinking much more in terms of long-range plans, recognizing our differences and needs."

There were 2,000 willing volunteers, young and old, who took part in the planning and execution of the centennial. At the heart of it was the centennial committee which worked hard for two years, says John. "They were determined in their views, but they were also good-humored. They were long-distance runners. I'm grateful for the chance to have worked with them."

Toward the end of the centennial year, as John and the committee were distributing to charitable enterprises the substantial surplus funds from their celebrations, John suddenly found himself in the hospital for a heart by-pass operation. As he recovered, his doctor said to him one day, "The stress of the last two years' hard work you put into the centennial probably contributed to this happening."

When he reported this to Denise, John added, "If it helped the city come together, I wouldn't have had it any other way."

Linda Davis, assistant superintendent, thinks Bockhorst is on the right track. Recently an elementary school teacher asked a long-time Pasadena resident to speak to a class about the city's Centennial. "It was amazing how the children responded," she said. They wanted to know how people lived without television and all the things they live with now. . . ."

John Wood little suspected that the making of this seemingly uncontroversial product would stir violent conflict, but he found himself in between three determined people—Elbie Hickambottom, a member of the school board, and the film-makers, George McQuilkin and Paul Bockhorst.

Elbie Hickambottom is a robust figure, energetic and outspoken. In his early 60s, he retains a military bearing, a legacy of his professional army career—a major at the time he returned to civilian life. A vigorous champion of the rights of his Black community and a member of the school board for the past ten years, he felt the centennial video had to be sensitive to the Black community's contribution to the city.

He recalls, "During the centennial, the city decided to have a video made as part of the celebration to show the history of Pasadena and it was previewed by the public in near-completed form. What I saw upset me, as it did some other Blacks in the community. We were faced with a difficult task—to communicate in an understandable way what our concern was so that others would be willing to do something about the film.

"I was also determined that if this film were going to be shown in our school district as part of our curriculum, changes would have to be made. I felt strongly that it lacked emphasis on the part of Blacks in the history of Pasadena and with the large number of minorities attending our schools, I knew it was very important for them not only to see accurately the involvement of their parents and grandparents, but also to understand that everything hadn't been peaches and cream."

At one time, said Elbie, Blacks were refused entrance to certain places. Until he was ten, only one theater was open to him as a boy in Pasadena. Even in that theater the Blacks were segregated and had to sit on the left in the front ten or 15 rows. When he was a youngster, his parents couldn't eat in a restaurant. Elbie wanted this discrimination alluded to in the film so that the young people could see how progress had been made.

Minorities had played a definite part in that change, and he wanted the younger generation to understand how restaurants had been opened to all races—not because the majority said, "Well, it's time for us to stop discriminating," but because Blacks took positive steps to cause that to happen. It wasn't through breaking restaurant windows or violent acts, but by appealing to the city directors, through discussion and, in time, by filing legal action that all this improvement had come.

Hickambottom went into action in his typical two-fisted manner, writing John a letter in which he voiced his objections to the film, charging "subtle racial overtones pervasive throughout the film." After sending copies of the letter to civic leaders, he scheduled an interview with the *Star-News* which headlined his charges the next day.

When John received Hickambottom's letter and read his outburst in the press, he thought to himself, "This isn't fair. We've gone to great length to record graphically in the video the painful injustices done to minorities in Pasadena throughout its history—not only to the Black community but the Japanese, Hispanics and others. What is it that Elbie is driving at?"

John telephoned a mutual friend who pointed out that though many of the historical injustices to the Black community had been corrected, the painful memories were very much still alive.

As a first step toward reconciling their differences, John invited Elbie to his home a few evenings later to meet with the video committee. He recalls, "Elbie talked heatedly of his concerns about the film for about an hour before anyone could get a word in." One participant of the evening remarked about John's uncanny ability to be kind and thoughtful, but at the same time firm.

What John discerned that evening in listening to Elbie was that at the root of his concerns was the failure of the film to demonstrate that it was the Blacks themselves who had taken the actions—which had corrected the injustices over the years. Elbie wanted minority children who would see this video in the schools to realize that in future years they themselves could take positive action to free their peoples from injustices.

When John later met with the video committee, he asked them, "Do you think that we could add this one ingredient to the film without violating the artistic integrity of the creators of the film?" Both Bockhorst and McQuilkin said they felt it was not only possible but right to do this. John returned to Elbie and described this concession, and Elbie agreed this addition was essentially what he wanted.

"Paul Bockhorst was the writer, director and producer of the film," says Elbie, "and he and I would have had some unresolvable differences if John had not played the role in reconciling us and getting the film back on track. Paul maybe didn't realize what the perspective of Blacks would be. He was very upset when he found that I was unhappy. The idea of going in and changing his film—and he had done a good job—left him very reluctant.

"I don't know what John said to Paul, but I know what he said to me. After a couple of meetings with me, interspersed with meeting Paul, he arranged for Paul and me to meet together. I was really apprehensive, but John had prepared us both so when it happened we were both ready to listen. In the beginning I felt like banging the table and saying, 'How could you show this in the film?' But I didn't. Instead I found myself willing to discuss the issues calmly and quietly. He was the same way. So the film was completed with the changes.

"I work with John and Denise on committee assignments, but I would like to say I appreciate having time just talking to them on a personal level, because they seem to have a faith that people can change and grow. If you really believe that, it gives you something to work toward. I'm not sure I believe that about older people. It's going to be very difficult for me, without some help, to work with a guy I think is a racist."

George McQuilkin is head of Churchill Films, one of Hollywood's most prestigious documentary film companies. Engaging and articulate, he sips coffee at breakfast and describes his part in the production of the video film of Pasadena's history.

"Some two years ago I was invited to a breakfast down at the clubhouse and there met John Wood, the centennial's director, Pat Bond and Tom Brannigan who was head of publicity. The object of the meeting, it turned out, was to draft me as a volunteer to oversee the making of the video on Pasadena. They had an outline of the film, but didn't have a producer, funding or anything else. Their idea was to have something 25 minutes long. It eventually grew to be a 90-minutes film, costing around $100,000. What I liked about it was the attempts to bring all of Pasadena together."

McQuilkin kept mulling over that. Clearly one of the objectives would be to deal with the different racial backgrounds. It would also be interesting to include a number of familiar objects—architectural features. Then one day as he swung around a street corner downtown and ran into the crowds of people, he said, "Ah! That's what it's about!" The history was the people of Pasadena, the ethnic groups, the waves of migration that settled the city, the wealthy people from the Midwest, the Japanese, the Black and the

Hispanics.

"So we hired a film-maker who we thought would be sensitive to those issues, Paul Bockhorst. It would have been easy to do a film on the wealthy and famous, the Rose Parade and the Valley Hunt Club and the mansions along Orange Grove Boulevard. We got together a committee to advise us, including different racial representatives and went to great pains to display the ethnic diversity. When the film was completed, all but the final scrubbing, it was shown at the Pasadena Playhouse and had a very strong positive response. The mayor said he thought it was wonderful. Some member of the school board said he felt like standing up and shouting hooray!

"But then came Elbie Hickambottom's outburst. After the premiere he had come up and said, 'Very good job.' There were a few little things that he wanted to discuss sometime. But in the next 24 hours those little things came to a boil. Two days later he was quoted in the newspaper as saying the film was racist and didn't represent the Black people."

When McQuilkin tried to talk to Elbie about it on the phone, he had to listen for 20 minutes—holding the phone about ten inches from his ear. Elbie had 26 points.

McQuilkin was at the initial gathering at the Woods' home and recalls it vividly: "I thought, this is going to be very, very difficult to resolve, because we're not talking about rational, discussable objectives, we're tackling something very deep. Elbie went into a big harangue and wouldn't listen to anyone, including the Black woman who had been on our committee and was a senior official in the education department. After two hours of being harangued and having my intentions and my hard work vilified, I came away from that meeting very depressed. I went home and told my wife, 'It'll never work.' "

McQuilkin said he had always thought that he was a person of great patience, but John Wood exceeded him ten-fold for he somehow tapped that core in people. He didn't just listen to the words on the surface. He listened to the center from which they were coming and seemed to try to decide whether it was said with reason. With Elbie John was able to listen to the 26 points, but then together they whittled them down to three or four which Elbie agreed were at the core of the main problem.

"With this toehold," McQuilkin recalls, "John saw there was some place where Elbie's objections and our needs could find a little common ground. It was a very difficult tactic to pursue. He had to listen to Elbie, but also defend Paul's and my right to artistic integrity. Yet there was never a sense of 'politically it would be wise, George, to change this part and then Elbie would drop his objections.' It was always, 'Could we, within the integrity of the film, do something which would meet everyone's approval?'

"My sense is that John, without losing sight of the goal, believes in the process even more than the results. Most people who want to bring about change have their eye on the goal; everything else is an obstacle to get around, or something to be manipulated in order to achieve their goal. John never loses sight of the process—and the process is people.

I've noticed that he secretly revels in the idea of bringing together people with opposing points of view, and then finding some common way that they can all work together."

He himself had been transformed watching John work, admits McQuilkin. Just as in the skills center project where John understood that if all they achieved was their goal, while in the process they alienated some individuals, these people would never participate in the process again. In the case of this film, the experience had brought the various factions a different understanding—which might be more significant than the showing of the film if it made the people involved stronger community participants than ever.

"Elbie could not have stood in the way of our completing the film," says McQuilkin. "We had the power, the money and the contacts. But he could have tainted the film. The controversy would have prevented it from reaching the community fully through the rental stores and book stores. People would have said, 'That's the video the Black community doesn't think is fair,' and it probably would not have been shown in the schools.

"The way we all got together, just as the people did over the skills center instead of defending their own turf, can be a great example for the country. Pasadena is a microcosm of America with its long-standing institutions and organizations, its very wealthy, its Black and Hispanic populations and its immigrants from across the border—many of whom are here illegally. If our people can solve the problems here, then maybe they're solvable in other places."

Paul Bockhorst sits at lunch in the restaurant of Brookside Park Clubhouse, close by the Rose Bowl, and philosophizes about his production of the video documentary. "I'm always interested in situations— whether they're in personal relationships or groups, that provide an opportunity to move beyond the superficial attitudes to touch something more basic, more real. That happened dramatically in my involvement with Elbie Hickambottom during the making of the Pasadena video, when he expressed his criticisms of it so forcefully.

"George McQuilkin and I responded in a similar way. He said to me, 'Paul, we've got to be clear where we stand. We've got to establish some lines here, and not be pushed around. Let's sit down and talk about our principles.' Integrity was important to both of us."

But, as the dialogue with Elbie continued, it occurred to Bockhorst that there was something more important than standards. Sometimes our principles can get in our way and it simply becomes more important to listen to people then to hold on to cherished ideals. John's behavior gave Paul an opportunity to discover other possibilities within himself, he admitted, for it dawned on him there was something more important here than the fate of one video production, and he began to understand there was a vital process being played out that involved the racial health of Pasadena.

"I saw that Hickambottom's views had an importance for the community at large. What Elbie was doing here was peeling back the normal social veneer of Pasadena and showing us the kind of world that had existed in the community for a very long time. I felt that the wound—the recognition that it was there—affected everyone, Black and white alike. And that was more important than the fate of the production. I could be grateful that Elbie's response to the video had made an opportunity to address the wound.

"What impressed me about John during that period when Elbie and other Black leaders were hacking the production in a seemingly merciless way was that he did not even appear to be offended and touchy about it. Most people would have taken the highly charged comments in a personal manner—for example, in Elbie's letter there was an accusation of racial corruption. I took that personally—and felt unappreciated because I had lost two jobs in the 60s as a result of trying to combat racism."

Further, said Bockhorst, John had a big stake in the production. The criticisms could have put him in a difficult position as chair of the coordinating committee, which had put a lot of money into the video. Also the future of the video was at risk, since its use in the city's schools could have been canceled.

He adds, "John and Denise are uniquely able to embrace a very wide range of people. They can relinquish control and ambitions. One can do that only if there is an inner trust. If you are fearful, you don't stand on a strong foundation. They are extraordinary in this culture, where competition, power, winners and losers are emphasized."

Paul Bockhorst wrote to Elbie Hickambottom and his wife after the controversy about the video had been resolved:

June 6, 1987

The main thing I want you to know is how much I value our dialogue regarding the depiction of black history in "Pasadena: A Heritage to Celebrate." It's been an extremely important experience for me. In fact, it has helped strengthen my faith in the ability of human beings to resolve important differences, even in the case of conflicts with deep historical roots. When your criticisms first surfaced, I was both angry and defensive. I took your charges personally and felt unjustly accused. And because I thought I had something to defend, it was hard for me to listen in an open-minded way to the *substance* of your concerns.

The experience of coming to recognize something beneficial in what I had previously perceived as a "threat" or an "attack" was of great significance and will surely benefit me for the rest of my life. I learned that it is often more important to listen with an open mind—and an open heart—than to self-righteously cling to some pre-existing position, no matter how deeply held. If I don't listen, then I can't learn new things, and without learning there is no possibility of growth, much less of reconciliation.

Another important aspect of the controversy surrounding the centennial video relates to the problems of racism. I've long been saddened by the racial divisions and antagonisms of Pasadena. They are all the more burdensome because they're so rarely acknowledged or discussed in public. And since there are so few chances to get the problems out into the open, where they could be addressed, they fester beneath the surface, damaging everyone, Black and white alike. . . . Well, this incident provided an opportunity to look beneath the deceptive surface, to see that all is not well and that much remains to be done to improve the city's racial climate.

To some people our dispute might seem like a small matter, a trivial footnote in the racial history of Pasadena. To me, it was profound in the true sense of the word. I say that because it provides a valuable model for how to handle highly charged racial matters, and that model could ultimately benefit a great many people. Instead of drawing lines and retreating behind defensive positions, we made an honest effort to listen to one another, to find out what was really at issue and how much room there was for negotiation. It was not an easy process, and a number of heated words were exchanged along the way. But we persevered, and in the course of our dialogue we came to respect each other's experiences and convictions, different though they were.

Contrary to our early suspicions, we discovered that all the parties were acting in good faith. What's more, we learned to like and respect one another as the unique individuals we really are. And in the end, we even came to an agreement on how to resolve our major differences. . . . If other disputes and tensions in the community could be handled in a similarly open and responsible manner, then Pasadena would be as exemplary in the area of human relations as it is in the spheres of science, architecture and higher education.

With sincere appreciation,
Paul Bockhorst

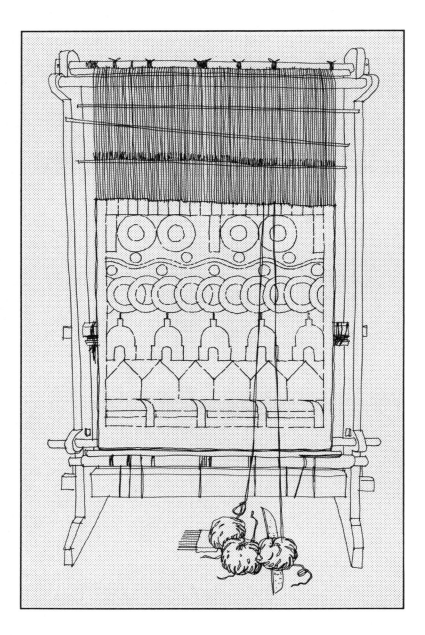

11

A Voice for the Children

Pasadena's centennial celebrations had provided both John and Denise an occasion to embark on prominent responsibilities in the life of the city. John's role as chair of the steering committee called forth all his diplomatic skills if the event were to prove a uniting process for the whole community. Denise also was challenged towards the end of the preparations for the celebrations when she was asked to join a committee charged with the task of selecting one of the five lasting gifts which the centennial found it was able to make to the city out of surplus funds.

Bessie Shenk, the centennial's corporate secretary, chaired this committee and she recalls the lively discussions among its members: "Ours was the education subcommittee, so of course we wanted the gift to be for children. I think it was Susan Caldwell who had the idea of a city commission being formed to look into the needs of children in Pasadena. It was an urgent concern and it was just the kind of thing I wanted. There were others on the committee who had different ideas, but in the end we prevailed.

"It was significant that only one other city in California had such a commission. Why was such a commission needed? There was great value in the people who were involved in the care of children getting to know one another and the work they were doing. Also, the main purpose of the commission was to learn the needs of our children and to make clear recommendations to the city directors for action."

Their proposal was accepted by the centennial committee and on July 21, 1986, the commission to study the needs of Pasadena's children was established by the city directors funded initially by a $15,000 gift from the centennial. Denise Wood was chosen its chair and found herself at the head of a dozen veteran professionals drawn from many areas of the city—representatives of each of the city's seven districts, the school board, police, people with experience in mental health problems, child abuse, handicapped children, child care agencies, and so on. Most of them were people whom she had come to know through her Office for Creative Connections activities.

"Pasadena is now thinking much more of long-range plans and realizing that we have changed," says Bessie Shenk. "Some people, (like me!) are abrupt in the way they want to change things. Denise appreciates people and carries them along with her and gets things done."

For Denise, however, chairing the commission was something beyond her experience. "First of all," she says, "the commissioners were not a united group coming together to address a single need. They were gathering under a common umbrella, but each brought different priorities with them. Individual commissioners felt they had to represent the interests of their constituencies as different needs and concerns were brought before the whole group. Otherwise, as one of the commissioners put it, 'I would lose all credibility with my own people.' "

It was also, Denise admits, a challenge to her style of leadership to work within the requirements of the Brown Act (which states that any meeting in California where there is a quorum of commissioners is required by law to be open to the public), and of having to post in city hall and the central library the agenda of the next meeting 72 working hours before it took place.

The group was rich and divergent in experience: some were skilled and trained in orderly procedure, others in speaking out for the voiceless at every point and at any cost. Yet ultimately the commission would have to speak with one voice to address the city directors and come to a consensus, both about priorities and about recommendations. There was one further complication: many commissioners were eager to "go public" so that everyone would know the commission existed. Yet it needed the first 16 months to gain trust and understanding for one another and to do the patient work of careful research from which would come focused recommendations and action.

Police Commander Bruce Philpott affirmed the importance of establishing the commission at this time. "There are many city commissions in Pasadena, but for the most part they are instruments for fine-tuning issues," he says. "This commission on children is different. It is addressing a need that has not been addressed. In Pasadena we may have an excess of committees and commissions, but the city board must have bodies that make recommendations to them. The importance of the care and education of children is now being recognized, and I think the findings of this commission will be laid before the Board at a very crucial time for its action."

Frank Jameson, director of Youth Services for the Pasadena Police Department, became the staff person for the Commission on Children—the first time the police department agreed to staff a commission. Denise had interviewed him before writing *Experiencing Pasadena* and at that time he had said to her, when she showed her concern about disadvantaged young people, "Don't get into it unless you're ready to do it for five years."

Jameson, a tall, robust and genial person whose field is child abuse and neglect, has an office in the police headquarters crowded with dolls, teddy bears, children's games and intriguing packages, piled on desks and chairs and around the walls. Should you walk in and look surprised, Jameson explains, "Sorry about the mess. Kids who are removed from their homes in a crisis are brought here first. I make sure that each one goes off to their temporary shelter with something to clutch in their arms." In 1984 he became one of the first of the twelve community advisors for the Office for Creative Connections.

He says about Denise, "As I got to know her I noticed several things: First, her tremendous ability to articulate her thoughts, but also to translate other people's thoughts into mutually understandable terms. Second, her obvious respect for the opinions of others (a unique gift!) and along with that, her ability to listen to what someone is saying to her and recognize its importance. Finally, her concern for the issues she was tackling."

In reflecting on the importance of the Commission for Children and Youth, Frank Jameson says you must understand that although there are a couple of dozen city commissions on different matters, Denise and Susan Caldwell, both members of the Centennial Lasting Gifts Task Force, helped conceive the idea of this one. It is just beginning to make an impact on the city for its mere existence is a statement to the community that there is enough concern about children in Pasadena to have a commission. "When I was addressing the coordinating committee of the centennial, I said, 'I just want kids to attain the status of sewers and gutters.' It is one of the few city commissions on the status of children in the state and I believe it will have a big impact."

When asked why there are only two city commissions on children in California, he says, "We talk a lot about children, but in terms of public policy I can't think of an issue that's further back on the bus than kids. It's almost always the last item on the budget to be served. That's what we want to reverse. Kids are disenfranchised. Program people can represent them, but they can be very easily deterred.

"This commission is a very fragmented group of 13 strong-willed individuals. Denise's job was to get us all lined up in a row to go over that narrow bridge—focusing on a collective agenda to be presented to the authorities."

Jameson feels the central issue is that program people in any field tend to be preoccupied with the survival of their own agency and many of them are competing for the same funding sources, so they defend their own turf. "Denise has brought people together in a bigger context—not to talk about their programs, but about larger issues that everyone can identify with—that tie into the goals these agency people have declared to be theirs. She has also made effective use of her friendship with community leaders—getting them to bring agency people together."

He adds, "It's very effective when the mayor or the superintendent of schools invites you to something. You attend! Another thing Denise does, which is very important for those of us involved in child care, is that she supplies us with recognition and support. Ours is a very stressful type of work and it takes a heavy toll in nervous complaints and breakdowns. We get burned out, and that support means a lot to us."

In the succeeding weeks the city directors agreed to fund a full-time staff person. (Because of his police work, Frank Jameson had only been able to give four hours a week). So after two years the Commission on Children and Youth became an established city commission, no longer at risk of being "sundowned," and well on its way. Publicly, the commission announced it was preparing a policy on children and youth which in 1989 it would ask the city directors to adopt—which put the community on notice that a committed group of advocates for children's needs was at work and a part of the city government's life.

In October 1989, at a regular meeting of the city board of directors, the commission presented "A Status Report on Pasadena's Children" and "A Proposed City Policy on Children, Youth and Families." The council chamber was crowded with people representing all sections of the community—many of whom were known for their substantial contributions to the well-being of children and youth.

The status report, well researched and summarized through a slide presentation, dramatized the stark reality of the needs of the city's children, youth and families: 55 percent of Pasadena's children live in the most economically depressed areas of the city; fully 44 percent of children in the public schools are eligible for the subsidized school lunch program; despite the ever-present teenage pregnancies, there are only 16 infant-care slots available to the 22,000-student unified school district—a lack which assures a high percentage of school dropouts among the young mothers.

The presentation of the status report was then backed by 17 urgent proposals, ranging from expanding quality child care to providing family housing, to affirming cultural diversity, to creating a healthy city, to encouraging youth participation and to financing the policy. The commission declared that its intent was to lay the groundwork for a vision and renewed commitment by the city to all its children and young people. It recommended the development of a ten-year plan with short- and long-range goals, with the aim that by the year 2000 Pasadena will have earned the reputation of being a "Family Community."

Director Katie Nack made the motion to accept the report, including its proposals, in its entirety. For half an hour a tight debate was waged, chiefly over the issue of the difficult-to-foresee cost of the policy. Gradually the importance of the goals gained acceptance and when the mayor called for a vote, it was unanimous in favor.

The hard work of deciding priorities among the proposals still lay ahead, but a landmark choice had been made by the community. The children had at last found a voice.

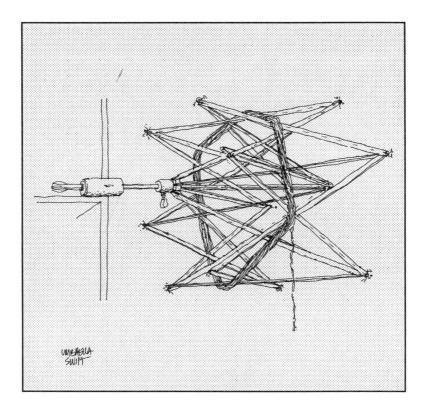

UMBRELLA
SWIFT

12

DAY ONE—Without Drugs

By 1985 the *Los Angeles Times* was calling Southern California "the world's largest retail market for cocaine." A young person in Pasadena had little difficulty through drug dealing accumulating the $10,000 needed to buy a Cadillac. Besides, the close links between gangs and drug dealing increasingly were becoming apparent.

By the fall of 1987 it was clear to Denise and five other leaders in the community that a strongly coordinated effort was needed to meet this epidemic which had reached Pasadena. Community awareness lagged far behind the growing dimension of the problem. The closest collaboration of everyone in both Pasadena and the adjoining town of Altadena would be needed for the young drug dealers ranged easily across the municipal line between Pasadena and Altadena and had become skilled at getting around the jurisdictional formalities of two law enforcement departments.

The group of five friends were highly knowledgeable about substance abuse: Bruce Philpott had been loaned by the police department to the city manager's office to oversee the start of the revitalization plan for the Northwest. Capable and approachable, he not only brought a sense that city hall genuinely wanted to improve life in the Northwest, but from his experience with the devastating power of drugs, he was deeply convinced that they were totally debilitating to any renewal plans the community might devise. Ibrahim Naeem, director of the Pasadena-Foothill branch of the Los Angeles Urban League, was a seasoned, cultured person who was convinced more comprehensive action was needed because too often unemployment figures were tied to drug usage figures. Ed Turley, tireless, blunt, street smart, worked in Altadena for the Los Angeles County Community Youth Gang Services doing most of his work through the night hours—trying to keep gangs from warring with each other while re-establishing the control parents had lost over their teenagers. Fran Neumann, full of vitality and skilled in communicating, with 25 years of outreach experience behind her, was the substance abuse consultant to the Office for Creative Connections who had just completed a survey for them of resources and needs connected with illegal drugs and alcohol abuse in Pasadena/Altadena. Lillian Rodriguez put in a 60-hour week as director of *El Centro de Accion Social.* and knew how drug abuse destabilized family life and ravaged the work she was trying to do day after day.

These five realized that any attempt to raise community-wide awareness would be a bold enterprise. Denise consulted Denis O'Pray from All Saints and began describing the urgency, danger and enormity of the drug problem with its links to the crime world. As her words poured out, Denis listened and then replied quietly, "I get the feeling you are going to do something about this. Rest assured, we'll back you to the hilt!"

The first step in the Office for Creative Connections' effort to mobilize a whole community was creating a community-wide awareness of the problem of substance abuse. The program they launched was called DAY ONE and the founders knew from experience that there was widespread community denial, even among churches and parents, of the extent of the use of illegal drugs and the abuse of alcohol, and that the general public felt powerless and immobilized by the size and viciousness of the problem, while professionals knew how high recidivism after treatment could be and how demoniac was the power of drugs.

Realizing some group needed to take a broad, coordinated responsibility, they looked for well-known individuals in the community who could provide united leadership to such a project. In 1987 began the first phase of the huge task of mobilizing a community to face up to and to turn back the onslaught of illegal drugs and the abuse of alcohol. One requirement for the venture was that it include resources already well established in Pasadena's life—the Council of Alcoholism and Drug Dependency, the grass-roots initiative of Citizens for a Drug Free Youth and the county-funded substance abuse center in the Northwest—among others.

As the initial plan took shape, the group took pains to bring on board the mayor, the chief of police, the city manager, the president of the board of education, the superintendent of schools and the head of the ecumenical council. Later a full fledged advisory council came into being which included the leadership of the chambers of commerce and of the NAACP in both communities and the Commission on Children and Youth. Twice a year they were briefed on DAY ONE's progress and asked their advice.

By consulting with the community, it was decided there would be four action groups representing basic needs. They were: 1) Treatment and Rehabilitation—making both accessible and affordable; 2) Education/Public Information—reaching schools and employers with input essential to mount a response to alcohol and other drug use within their organizations; 3) Law Enforcement/Safe Neighborhoods—enabling citizens to feel better able to communicate with their police force and regain control of their neighborhoods; and 4) Alternative Activities for Youth—coordinating recreational, vocational and leadership opportunities which were in existence for young people of the community and also including young people in future planning.

The founding group invited gifted professionals to co-chair each of the four groups. All who were asked accepted and they gathered to forge a name for their operation. DAY ONE was chosen with its twin themes: Take charge of your life and take care of your community. Its purpose was to choose wellness, to start over again and build something new.

Two tests faced such a bold initiative: would people respond by getting involved and would there be adequate funding?

Kaiser Permanente Medical Group which had recently moved its headquarters into the city was truly farsighted and funded a grant request to cover the first three years of all administrative costs. Their chief executive officer, Hugh Jones, said to Denise, "Thank you for coming to us. You helped us get out into the community," The Pasadena *Star-News* devoted its lead editorial of April 28, 1989 to celebrate the gift with a headline, "Day one for DAY ONE—Drug Abuse Fight looks to the Future."

> Sixty or 70 community leaders from Altadena and Pasadena gathered on a hot spring morning yesterday to make a commitment to the future. The mayor was there, the city manager, police chief, school board members, Pasadena City College board members, the head of the NAACP, ministers, chamber of commerce reps—important people in these towns. But important people gather every morning. This was different, and everyone who was there knew it. They were talking about it. They were excited about the possibilities they were helping to create. It was the official day for DAY ONE, a mobilization of the two communities created to address the abuse of drugs and alcohol. Its theme: "Take charge of your life, take care of the community." Who has a better theme than that?

DAY ONE has been organizing for a year now, but you probably haven't heard about it. Its leaders have kept quiet while funding and organizational strategies were developed. Yesterday's meeting at the East Walnut Street headquarters of Kaiser Permanente was held to announce that the major funding has been secured, to the tune of a three-year $200,000 grant from Kaiser. The generous donation from this relatively new-to-the-area corporate citizen will pay for all administrative costs through mid-1991 as DAY ONE swings into action.

DAY ONE co-chair Denise Wood—called "our beacon and our conscience" by Charles McKenney in his introduction—put the reason for the groups' existence very simply in an eloquent talk. DAY ONE is around so that drug and alcohol abusers "Can live the healthy lives they deserve to lead," she said. There's no reason to get highfalutin' about it. Healthy lives are what it is all about.

DAY ONE will not run drug abuse programs or services itself, although it may help create them as needed. Instead, it will be a catalyst and organizer of others in the community. A synergy will be created among the corporate, educational, law enforcement and religious communities.

Four action groups from among DAY ONE volunteers will concentrate on alternate activities for youth, education/public information, law enforcement/ safe neighborhoods and treatment/rehabilitation. A particular emphasis will be put on encouraging old fashioned nosy neighbors who will not allow drug dealers to take over neighborhoods, plying their trade in the open.

And that funny name? Wood says, "Suppose it's five years in the future, and we have been successful.

We'll say 'Be careful—it's still just day one' in the struggle to lead healthy, productive lives."

Each of the four action committees went to work. The treatment/rehabilitation group from the start had a grassroots resource of incalculable value: the twelve-step approach of Alcoholics Anonymous.

A.A. has a 50-year track record of helping people achieve and maintain sobriety and its methods have proven to be effective as well for those addicted to cocaine and other narcotics. A.A. also offers a remarkable support system for the families of users; however, some cases of addiction require medical intervention before the twelve-step method can take over. Since 30 days in an inpatient hospital program can cost $18,000 or more, affordable insurance and more free beds are urgently needed.

The treatment/rehabilitation members' first step was obvious and simple, but had not been tried before. They gathered the heads of the local treatment centers in one room where they could meet as a group and start planning together and also listen as the need for free beds was presented to them. One by one 14 were offered and the Council on Alcoholism and Drug Dependency volunteered to be the clearing house for a fair allocation of these beds.

By the spring of 1989, the search for affordable, accessible health insurance coverage was a main concern of the treatment/rehabilitation group. It was also in the process of designing a complete community "system of care" which will include sober centers, places where families, kids as well as recovering persons can enjoy themselves without the temptation of alcohol or other drugs.

The education/public information subgroup began its outreach through the chamber of commerce to speak to the city's employers. A new federal law required a drug-free workplace of all companies engaged in business connected to national security. This affected certain employers, notably the Jet Propulsion Laboratory (JPL) and the California Institute of Technology (Caltech), who brought their representatives to the workshops co-sponsored by the chamber of commerce and DAY ONE.

At the other end of the spectrum, 90 percent of Pasadena's companies employ ten workers or less and these needed an affordable employee assistance program to care for any of their personnel requiring drug-related education or wanting substance-abuse rehabilitation. This whole workshop initiative required a very modest funding because of the cooperation of the chamber, the local treatment centers and the participants and DAY ONE—making for an all-around better use of resources already available in the community.

The law enforcement/safe neighborhoods subgroup meetings seemed to generate the most heat for there was so much pent-up frustration and fear in individuals in the community wanting to be heard. Neighborhood leaders came to these meetings to ask pressing questions: Why was the person on the switchboard at police headquarters sometimes rude and abrupt? Why did it take so long to put a drug dealer behind bars? Why couldn't the sheriff of Los

Angeles County (protecting Altadena) and the police of Pasadena get together better?

Month after month real issues were dealt with. One group went to see judges of the superior court to ask that jail sentences for dealers be made more severe. Another group began to look into the legal steps to be taken in order to hold absentee landlords accountable for drug dealings on their premises. Others scrutinized the list for new applications for liquor licenses posted in city hall in order to initiate a protest should such new facilities be too near a school or another location already having a liquor store. These were small but important steps, for gradually a sense of participation and responsibilities came into these neighborhoods; people no longer felt as powerless.

The alternative activities for youth action group faced what may have been the hardest task for they needed to increase the cooperation and communication between all those having any professional commitment with young people as well as involving the young people themselves—an important element in designing any workable plan for the future. This endeavor would also require better cooperation between the city's parks and recreation department and the school district, while coordination to help young people develop job skills, leadership skills and self-esteem would have to be nurtured.

Two goals were chosen: first, during the school year to train middle school and high school students in decision-making, self-esteem and leadership, and second, during the summer time, to undertake activities with young people that provided recreation in the community and camping experiences and took some of the high-risk youth out of their environment for a week at a time. A team of counselors composed of people from various youth agencies in Pasadena was made available so when the young people came back from camp they could remain connected with those who would be ready to support them at home, since so many young people returned to a tempting and debilitating environment.

Out-of-door dances were also initiated to welcome young people from all over the city. This took courage considering the ever-mounting number of drive-by shootings which since January 1989 had broken all Pasadena records. Fortunately the dances went well and provoked no incidents. Those young people who had participated in putting on the dances began to show leadership in other areas—one group even formed their own support group.

The second phase of DAY ONE's contribution to Pasadena/Altadena came into focus in May 1989. In the face of the nationwide escalation of substance abuse a foundation took a far-reaching decision. The Robert Wood Johnson Foundation announced:

> . . . the availability of $26.4 million in grants to support intensive, community-wide initiatives to reduce the demand for illegal drugs and alcohol. The purpose of these community-wide initiatives is to demonstrate that by consolidating resources and creating a single community-wide system of prevention, early identification, treatment and after-care, communities can, over time, achieve substantial

reduction in the demand for—and consequently the use of—illegal drugs and alcohol. The proposed demand reduction activities would complement and reinforce ongoing efforts to reduce the illegal drug supply and to regulate the use of alcohol.

This Foundation program is intended for medium-sized U.S. communities—towns or cities with populations of approximately 100,000 to 250,000 persons—who are experiencing serious problems with drug and alcohol abuse.

DAY ONE's board of directors, the coordinating council and the community advisors together took the decision to respond to the Robert Wood Johnson Fighting Back initiative and apply for a one-year planning and development grant of $100,000.

The timing was extraordinarily propitious. Two years earlier DAY ONE had rolled up its sleeves and acquired unique practical experience. Under the imaginative and energized leadership of its executive director, Fran Neumann, it had created new partnerships in town and had united treatment and rehabilitation agencies to a new degree. Law enforcement personnel, health providers and a trio of public, private and parochial schools were pooling information and resources in a new way.

The clergy leadership in the Northwest had forged a consensus such as had not existed to such a degree before. The community at large was slowly becoming aware of the size of the drug and alcohol problem from the daily stories in the press and it was also aware that DAY ONE was committed to enabling both Pasadena and Altadena regain control of their quality of life.

In October word reached DAY ONE that although it had survived the first cut among the 333 applicants, it had not been one of the final winners of the Johnson award. Disappointing as this was, all the hard work that had gone into preparing the grant request soon paid off. The first two new sources which were approached—the City of Pasadena and Los Angeles County—between them gave the full $100,000. So DAY ONE entered a phase of being a trusted enabler and a practical catalyst.

13

Every Child's Right

While the DAY ONE undertaking was getting started, the leaders of the Office for Creative Connections, faithful to their conviction that basic community problems must be addressed on many fronts, pushed forward another probe. Lorna Miller, its associate director, undertook to discover the realities of health care for Pasadena children and young people from low-income families. Both she and Denise were deeply committed to the second recommendation in *Experiencing Pasadena* which urged that everyone's children must matter to the whole community.

For an entire year Lorna Miller went to talk one-on-one with the health providers, the parents and the school nurses in the greater Pasadena area using a basic questionnaire to document the addresses, hours, fees, access ramps for the handicapped and languages spoken at each site. All this information was transferred to the PALS system (Public Access Library

Service) at the Pasadena Central Library to make it available to the widest possible public.

Armenian by descent, Lorna, small of build, has an open and warm personality. Instinctively, people like and trust her. Soon she became an authority with an impressive overview of the needs and resources affecting the health of Pasadena's children. In addition to obtaining a thorough measure of the resources and gaps in services, she gained far more by always going in person to learn what were the realities.

A school nurse expressed the secret: "How amazing that someone from the community would care enough to come and see how I was getting on."

It became abundantly clear to Lorna that although there were many health resources in Pasadena, two conditions prevented people from fully using them: On the one hand payment for care was required and many family were too poor to pay for services and had no insurance. There was only one low-cost, walk-in clinic in the community which was open for two hours every Tuesday night at a community center in the Northwest. But whoever heard of a child getting sick on the right day! On the other hand few were aware of other low-cost services that were available.

Lorna compiled a report entitled, "The Health of Pasadena's Children," which immediately gained valuable public recognition. Pasadena's recently created Commission on Children and Youth added its support by funding the printing of the report in June 1988. The cover letter stated:

The Pasadena Commission on Children and Youth salutes the thoroughness and timeliness of this excellent report on health services for our community's youth. This is much more than a survey. Its well-researched content offers both information for resources as well as identification of problem areas. Consideration of health services necessarily involves several social issues which the report presents clearly, thereby enabling the reader to appreciate the subject in its larger context.

As advocates for the welfare of our young people and their families, the Commission hopes that the specific recommendations may serve as an agenda around which to rally community response. We must all be our children's voice to ask for and work for the assistance they may need, specially with an issue as crucial and complex as wellness.

Lorna next gathered a group of 16 leaders concerned with health-related issues. She and Denise met with them at two-hour working lunches, given by the Office for Creative Connections, four times in two months. This group included top-ranking people from the Huntington Memorial Hospital, the department of health, the health office of the school district, Pasadena Planned Parenthood, the Pasadena Commission on Children and Youth, the Junior League, the Child Care Coalition, DAY ONE and Pasadena Mental Health. The primary purpose was to decide together which of the needs shown up by the report should be addressed first.

Fully a fourth or more of the students in Pasadena public schools are without health insurance and therefore families need to have available to them not only low-cost clinics, but ones open after work hours for same-day appointments or on a walk-in basis.

Clearly many things needed to be done to increase accessibility and affordability of health care to all of Pasadena's children. The group decided to concentrate on helping where some services were already being provided and where the most children could be reached. It made sense to enhance the services offered by the school health offices in the Pasadena Unified School District. The district's 30 campuses are presently served by 15 full-time nurses and 25 part-time ones. But on many days there is neither a nurse nor a health clerk at an elementary school, for there are no funds available for hiring additional health personnel. A community response is needed.

Three strategies emerged:

1) To set up a network of well-coordinated volunteers who are trained to assist nurses with clerical work on mass testing days, with vision and hearing screening, with arranging transportation home for a sick child and with being supportive of students waiting to be picked up by parents.

2) To create a network of local pediatricians who could be available for telephone consultation and for providing medical services to students who do not have easy access to health care during school hours.

3) To enlist a network of mental health professionals who could be available for telephone consultation, for conducting group rap sessions for students on campus, for counseling individual students and so to meet an often expressed need for the young

people to be able to talk with adults who both had skills and time.

This group, for whom trust and friendship were such an important part of the mix—although they did not always agree with each other—turned out to be dynamic and imaginative. Creative problem-solving began to take place at their lunches. When Lorna and Denise asked the group whether it wished to stay together, they enthusiastically agreed to do so, taking the name of the Health Coalition for Children and Youth. The Office for Creative Connections was asked to be the convener of these new partnerships.

By May 1989 the Health Coalition for Children and Youth numbered 24 members. More doctors and mental health professionals had joined and the newly appointed head of the department of health became a permanent member. Then a fund-raiser came forward offering her services.

At a community luncheon on May 2, 1989, hosted by the coalition, speakers included the mayor, the deputy superintendent of schools, the head pediatrician of the Huntington Memorial Hospital and the head of the department of health.

The main speaker, Dr. Philip Porter, director of Healthy Children of Harvard University, gave convincing evidence from five other communities of how a broad-based, coordinated approach to health access can transform the supply of resources available to poor families. In his letter of thanks to Lorna afterwards he commented, "Pasadena is well on its way!"

Once again a need had been researched and documented, then a diverse group of professionals who were linked to the issue were invited to determine priorities and choose a practical strategy. Next, a coalition came into being creating its own energy. One of its members, a trustee of Pasadena City College, when asked how she could find time in her busy schedule to attend the monthly lunches and working committees so faithfully, answered, "It refreshes me to come here. Not only is this a place for the process to happen . . . it's a place where the vision is kept alive."

"Place" can have several meanings: an actual site, a mindset, a core of committed people. Month after month it was becoming apparent how crucial it was for there to be a "place" for the process to happen— of working together, of holding the vision, of renewal for the care-givers. Clearly this component is an important factor in any mobilizing of an entire community.

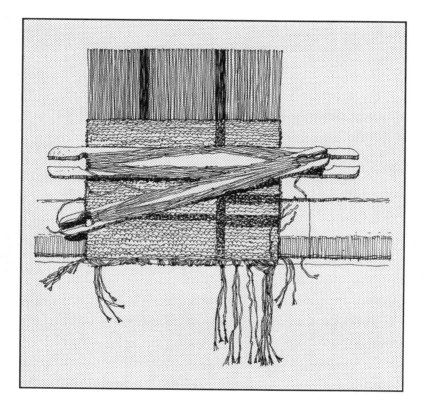

14

Conscience of a City

By the spring of 1989 John and Denise had decided to move back East to be nearer their family. After 17 years in Pasadena, they were leaving behind a legacy—gaining momentum under able leadership—of new enterprises to improve the quality of life of Pasadena: the Community Skills Center, the Office for Creative Connections, the Commission on Children and Youth, DAY ONE, the Health Coalition for Children and Youth.

Another gift they had given—expressed by many who had worked closely with them and knew at first hand their persistence, hard work and unflagging expectancy that things could be better—was an intangible feeling that they had enriched, empowered and energized people around them. Often these friends spoke about the Office for Creative Connections for it seemed to embody the distinctive way both Denise and John went about things.

Lorna's husband, Don Miller, tried to articulate what this commitment has produced: "In the process of listening to many different people, Denise first discovered that a lot of people in the city did not know that other people were thinking similar thoughts, or were involved in analogous activities. So an important part of her role was informally to connect people in the city.

"But maybe a more important thing that the Office for Creative Connections has done, beyond the round tables and conferences and coalitions, has been the nurturing of individuals within these agencies and services to the city. That caring begins with listening to people, finding out about their frustrations, but then goes on to supporting them in their hopes and ambitions. And that method, I think, has been transferred to others who work with Denise—to Lorna, for example, in the work she is doing right now on the youth health services.

"When you think about the structure of the city, there is really no one who plays a pastoral role for Pasadena. Cities tend to be divided into interest groups who are contending with each other for turf or power. So Creative Connections has been playing a unique role."

"I can testify to that," says Lorna. "When I first went out on interviews I used to ask Denise what questions I should ask. Denise always said, 'Let's see how you can 'feed' that person.' I would be going out to get information from them, but she would remind me of what I could give them. And somehow by the end of the interview the person would be talking about herself or himself, which was part of that nurturing. So much of that kind of research is done by sending out questionnaires, asking for information. But it's those in-between personal questions that people really respond to."

In Lorna's experience, this method of listening, before embarking on an interview or a program, was very important in giving people direction. She had just been at a meeting, for example, where a substance-abuse task force wanted to do something for parents without really knowing what the parents wanted or needed. It made so much more sense to talk to and listen to parents for a while before deciding what was most needed.

"Listening becomes a powerful tool in planning. Programs mean so much more when they come out of careful listening and assessment. And beyond that, when you get interested in people, the job gets done for you. You set something in motion."

"Yes," says Don. "The problem is not lack of organizations. Pasadena has 225 human-service agencies. It doesn't make sense to go out and create one more of them."

Looking back now at the start of the Office for Creative Connections, Don speculates that they must have felt the time was ripe to experiment with a different kind of approach. Historically the church had often adopted a more assertive stance trying to achieve social justice through conflict—making it just one more power player. Maybe all along they had been groping for a method where people could be helped to forget their differences and start to work together on a common task that was bigger than what was dividing them.

"We have seen that happen repeatedly," says Lorna. "Denise and I have been in groups where the meeting starts out with a big problem. By allowing people plenty of time, maybe over a weekly breakfast, they can discuss their frustrations or speak about their differences. We don't say, hide all that and get on with the task, but rather focus on the need, while allowing time for the off-loading. It is at this point you begin to see the tightness change to a feeling of wanting to cooperate. By the end of these sessions people are usually focused with a passion on how they can help with the problem—for example, 'How can we help these kids?' "

Michael Friedline of World Vision echoes the same theme. "Denise and John's work has been to build relationships. They have established an incredible network. Most people won't try to build personal relationships because they think it's too time consuming. They'd rather distribute flyers or send out announcements. Denise learned long ago that you need to spend time with people, first on the phone, then talking over agenda, and so on. Ultimately, building relationships one-on-one is not a waste of time. It's essential in order to achieve the goal."

Friedline says there's always been a common theme in their activities: justice, the reconciliation of people plus a sense of making the community a better place. They also participate in things that give people a sense of belonging and their projects are inclusive, providing a common goal for which people can come

172

together and get to know each other. Beyond this, Creative Connections works well because Pasadena is cohesive—it has a sense of its history, civic pride and churches with a social role."

Denis O'Pray of All Saints throws an interesting light on the Woods and their interaction with fellow Pasadenans: "I suppose there are a lot of people who could testify to the impact that John and Denise's style has had on them—which seems to have to do with creating a safe space in which one can explore one's best self, one's highest motives and one's deepest instincts, free from the need to be self-protective or competitive."

Bruce Philpott, now back in the Pasadena Police Department—one of three commanders and in charge of all the uniformed officers out in the field—looks at the Woods' work from a similar point of view: "Creative Connections came to Pasadena at a very relevant time, when people were beginning to be aware of our different community interests, and it has become to some extent the conscience of this city. We do not have the old blue blood leadership anymore. The demographic shift has happened so rapidly it has caused us to look at the traditional white dominated policies and ask who are we now? We see special interests promoting very narrow benefits, perhaps at the cost of greater concerns. For example, in general everyone is in favor of adequate housing, but when a proposal is made to provide institutional housing in someone's neighborhood, invariably the reaction is NIMBY—'not in my back yard!'

"Of course, in Pasadena we have a rather sophisticated way of processing controversy. We try to avoid confrontational methods, keeping issues from surfacing. But they are there—Black, Hispanic, dropout and unemployment issues. John and Denise Wood have a different way. They express and live a policy of not ostracizing your adversary on a personal basis. By doing so you lose communication and cannot close wounds, but rather cause scars. The Woods are change agents. They live to create a personal expression of concern—that we're only going to advance as a species by sharing love and respect for others. So they are on the cutting edge of change. And the Office for Creative Connections brings a sense of moral consciousness into our neighborhoods, churches, police, government and community."

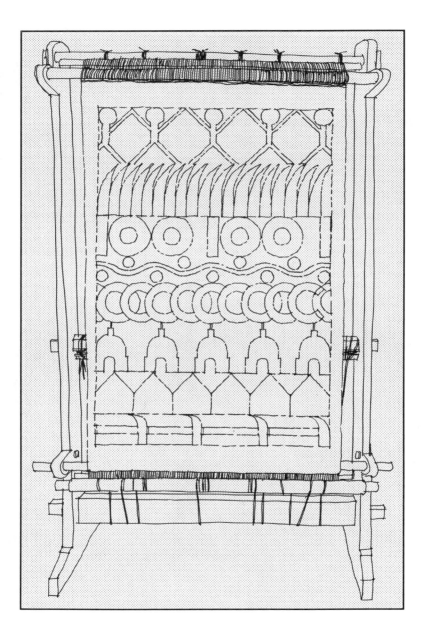

15

Resources and Guidelines

By the autumn of 1989 word of the Woods' forthcoming departure to the East Coast had spread through the community and on November 14 they were invited to the city hall. There Mayor William E. Thomson, Jr., at a meeting of the city board of directors, presented the Woods with a key to the city, whose inscription read:

> From the citizens of Pasadena, with our sincere appreciation for your unselfish commitment and dedication to improving the quality of life in this community.

As he made the award, the mayor said, "This is an occasion of recognition that brings to me and I am sure to all of us a combination of joy and of sadness. And that is for John and Denise Wood who have given more of themselves to this community and to all of us than probably we would dare hope for from any couple. . . .

"Earlier this year I had the pleasure of handing out a key to the city of Pasadena and made the comment that we don't often do that. In fact, other than that one time before, I don't remember ever doing it in the city. We thought a lot about what would be appropriate to give the two of you. We felt that as this is something we do seldom, it is the very thing to give the two of you, to remember us by and as a means of saying thank you most sincerely for your presence, for your love and for your many, many contributions to Pasadena."

Denise responded, ". . . I can only say that the 17 years John and I have lived in this city in your midst have been the richest experience of our lives. We've seen a city accept its diversity, we've seen a city welcome coalitions, and we've seen a city that is ready to build a new future for everybody together. And I think those of you who sit around this council area deserve a special place, because you are seriously wrestling to give their birthright to every child—and to every person—in this city. That is heroic and it is necessary."

John said, "We are greatly honored and we thank you so much. I believe that there is something of God in each person. Therefore it's important that we struggle to honor and uphold all the people of our city and that we honor and uphold one another in this struggle. These have been wonderful years for us. We have loved living in Pasadena. And we hope that all our friendships here will go on forever."

What has enabled John and Denise to accomplish all they have done? What prepared them for the part they have played in their community? When confronted with these questions, both hasten to explain that they had several things going for them for which they can claim no credit.

"Pasadena has a wealth of civic-minded people," says Denise, "who were deeply involved in volunteer work long before we appeared on the scene. And there were many more who only needed a little encouragement to jump in."

"Besides that," John adds, "there is a conscious heritage here, going back 100 years, that has maintained the city's identity, despite growth and diversity. That's a great help in mobilizing citizens to act.

"There was yet another resource in Pasadena," John reflects, "which prepared us for what we were to do. We had not been churchgoers most of our lives, but here we found a live and contemporary church, full of people of all ages and backgrounds. It oriented us towards the city and its needs. In it we have found friends and colleagues in our undertakings."

Denise interjects, "I would like to speak especially of two friends, Denis O'Pray and Don Miller, who helped shape the Office for Creative Connections and who gave John and me steadfast support and perspective for what we set out to do in those years. All Saints has nourished us and built upon the foundations in our lives."

And what were those foundations in their lives? John ventures an answer: There were many things. Denise inherited gifts of creativity and perspective from her father, a Boston inventor and head of an international manufacturing firm. And from her mother, a Paris-born woman of extraordinary vitality, Denise inherited both energy and courage.

As for John, his father, he says, was a well-loved Episcopal minister and theologian who died in a car accident when John was 18, "but by then he had planted in me the seeds of loving people and of loving God, though it took years for them to grow in me. My mother, who died last year at 96, has shown me a life of steadfastness, integrity and of wide-ranging compassion, the older she got."

But what in their own experience has especially developed their capacities for inspiring and mobilizing others? "Denise and I share the unique experience of having been, ever since college days, a part of Moral Re-Armament, a world-wide network of people of different races, religions and backgrounds working to bring God's dimension into the way people and nations live their lives.

"We worked full-time with them for 25 years on five continents and learned during this period something of doing big things together, seeing the greatness in each person and each culture, thinking for a whole city or a whole society and never giving up. We also learned to listen to what the other person is really thinking and even more important to listen to the voice inside us and to heed it.

"Another great experience for us was to be in on the creation and early years in the mid-60s of 'Up With People,' the innovative, international educational venture. Those years were full of travel, of reaching out to all sorts of audiences with this musical production, and of a reaffirmed confidence in the qualities of idealism and leadership there are in young people.

"One of our steadying resources," continues John, "has been that Denise and I can talk together. We take time most days to hear from each other what the other has been thinking and doing. We try to enter each other's work creatively and with encouragement, being real and realistic with each other. Sometimes, this means just listening. Other times it's to give back ideas. Often it's to sense where we are heading. This lends vitality to all we do."

Denise adds her perspective, "People are quick to agree that we live in a time of extraordinary transition, of technical marvel, of 'progress.' But I wonder whether, when people look back at our times, they won't say the distinctive mark was not so much the scientific marvels as the dawning in people's consciousness of what it means to be truly human."

By that she means people are realizing they need more than just success, more than what you can touch, see or smell; that they have an inner scale on which are weighed integrity and lasting values plus a sensitivity planted deep in the heart of every being—a recognition that each one can only go forward together with the rest of the human race.

"In my first book, *Experiencing Pasadena*," Denise adds, "I wrote about 'Green Shoots of Hope.' These were single individuals or a few people who saw a need and rolled up their sleeves and did something to address it. Obviously it takes huge efforts to bring about societal change, but the beginning of that larger change is marked by what the conscience and the courage of a few people helped them decide to try and do."

When pressed further to sum up the guidelines they have learned to pursue during their years in Pasadena, Denise refers to a remark made by their friend Police Commander Bruce Philpott: "John and Denise have a mindset. Others buy into it and start to use it. The story is what has resulted."

They spell out that mindset for cities as it has grown in their experience:

1. Hold to the expectancy and the determination that you and others can make a difference in your community.

2. Study the city by listening to its people one-by-one to gain a living picture of the city's needs, strengths and possibilities.

3. Reveal the city to itself—the pain, the facts, the hopes and the moral imperatives you have learned—not in name-calling and blaming, but neither in watering down the truth.

4. Think and speak for the whole city.

5. Bring people together, not in confrontation but in trust, to tackle the city's most urgent needs.

6. Build on the agencies and the people who are already at grips with a given issue and, where need be, encourage new initiatives and coalitions.

7. Take care of the care-givers of your community so they know they are not alone and can receive the citizens' support they need.

8. Aim to build lasting relationships.

9. Know there is more power in appealing to the very best in people rather than the worst.

10. Persist when everything seems to fall apart, conscious that it takes patience, perseverance and passion to move a city.

John has a last word. "Prepared or not, again and again since coming to Pasadena, Denise and I have found ourselves confronted with tasks that seemed beyond our experience and our capacity. We decided to run with those tasks, trusting that we would be taught how to accomplish them as we went. As we launched out, we found ourselves shoulder to shoulder with others who felt as we did. They were wonderful allies, often gifted and experienced for the tasks far beyond Denise and me. What we have done, others can surely do, and better than we."

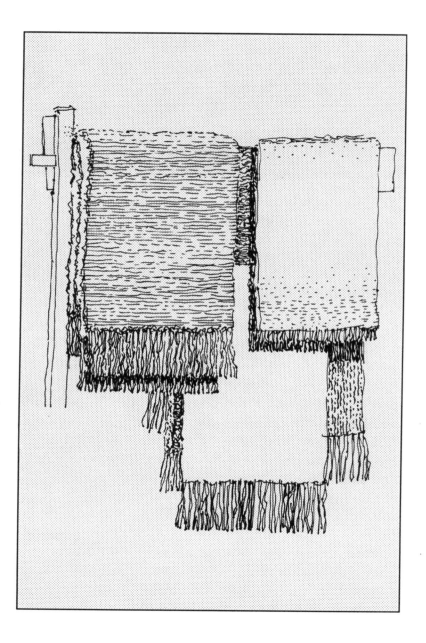

The author with Denise and John Wood.

Basil Entwistle graduated from Oxford University with first class honors in philosophy, politics and economics. He left a teaching career to work in the field of human and social development, spending eight years in Japan at the invitation of postwar leaders to participate in the country's democratic regeneration and authored *Japan's Decisive Decade*. During World War II he served in Europe at U.S. Air Force headquarters editing publications. In the 1960s he returned to education as founder and first chair of Mackinac College. He now lives with his wife in Santa Barbara, California.

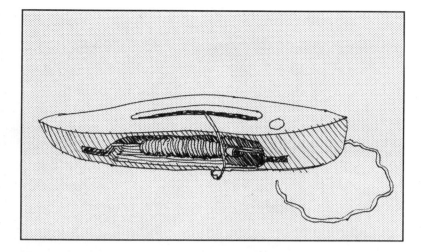

Illustrator **Patric Dawe** is an architect, city planner and Pasadena resident who has known John and Denise Wood since 1980 when he moved to Pasadena with his family. Pat worked with the Woods on the Pasadena Goals Congress in the early 1980s.

The drawings were done at Mission West Weavers in South Pasadena, a weaving studio and retail shop whose manager assisted Pat in assembling the weaving implements to tell a graphic story of weaving, reinforcing the Edna St. Vincent Millay quote.

The weaving which is shown in progress throughout the book illustrates the Woods' involvements in Pasadena.